CAMBRIDGE LIBRARY COLLECTION

Books of enduring

Women's

The later twentieth century saw a huge ↑
writing, which led to the rediscovery of
of genres, periods and languages. Many books that were immensely popular
and influential in their own day are now studied again, both for their
own sake and for what they reveal about the social, political and cultural
conditions of their time. A pioneering resource in this area is Orlando:
Women's Writing in the British Isles from the Beginnings to the Present
(http://orlando.cambridge.org), which provides entries on authors' lives and
writing careers, contextual material, timelines, sets of internal links, and
bibliographies. Its editors have made a major contribution to the selection of
the works reissued in this series within the Cambridge Library Collection,
which focuses on non-fiction publications by women on a wide range of
subjects from astronomy to biography, music to political economy, and
education to prison reform.

Strictures on the Modern System of Female Education

A unique and influential public figure in her time, Hannah More
(1745–1833) was a prolific writer. This two-volume study, published in
1799, is her definitive work on women's education and was enormously
successful, going through thirteen editions by 1826 and selling over
19,000 copies. The work outlines More's belief that women's education and
conduct determined the moral state of a nation, reflecting her acceptance
of eighteenth-century views on the status and education of women. In
Volume 1, a heavy emphasis is placed on the need for women to observe
propriety, and More argues that women should seek to acquire knowledge
and discipline rather than accomplishments. The modern reader will find
More's conservative stance on women's rights a fascinating contrast to more
liberal works of the age, including Mary Wollstonecraft's *A Vindication of
the Rights of Women* (also reissued in this series). For more information
on this author, see http://orlando.cambridge.org/public/svPeople?person_
id=moreha

[handwritten margin note: SEEMS PROGRESSIVE but is it really?]

Cambridge University Press has long been a pioneer in the reissuing of out-of-print titles from its own backlist, producing digital reprints of books that are still sought after by scholars and students but could not be reprinted economically using traditional technology. The Cambridge Library Collection extends this activity to a wider range of books which are still of importance to researchers and professionals, either for the source material they contain, or as landmarks in the history of their academic discipline.

Drawing from the world-renowned collections in the Cambridge University Library, and guided by the advice of experts in each subject area, Cambridge University Press is using state-of-the-art scanning machines in its own Printing House to capture the content of each book selected for inclusion. The files are processed to give a consistently clear, crisp image, and the books finished to the high quality standard for which the Press is recognised around the world. The latest print-on-demand technology ensures that the books will remain available indefinitely, and that orders for single or multiple copies can quickly be supplied.

The Cambridge Library Collection will bring back to life books of enduring scholarly value (including out-of-copyright works originally issued by other publishers) across a wide range of disciplines in the humanities and social sciences and in science and technology.

Strictures on the Modern System of Female Education

*With a View of the Principles
and Conduct Prevalent Among Women
of Rank and Fortune*

VOLUME 1

HANNAH MORE

CAMBRIDGE
UNIVERSITY PRESS

CAMBRIDGE UNIVERSITY PRESS

Cambridge, New York, Melbourne, Madrid, Cape Town, Singapore,
São Paolo, Delhi, Dubai, Tokyo

Published in the United States of America by Cambridge University Press, New York

www.cambridge.org
Information on this title: www.cambridge.org/9781108018906

© in this compilation Cambridge University Press 2010

This edition first published 1799
This digitally printed version 2010

ISBN 978-1-108-01890-6 Paperback

STRICTURES

ON THE

MODERN SYSTEM

OF

FEMALE EDUCATION.

VOL. I.

Domeſtic Happineſs, thou only bliſs
Of Paradiſe that has ſurviv'd the Fall!
Thou art not known where PLEASURE is ador'd,
That reeling Goddeſs with the zoneleſs waiſt.
Forſaking thee, what ſhipwreck have we made
Of honour, dignity, and fair renown!
                              COWPER.

STRICTURES

ON THE

MODERN SYSTEM

OF

FEMALE EDUCATION.

WITH

A VIEW OF THE PRINCIPLES AND CONDUCT PREVALENT
AMONG WOMEN OF RANK AND FORTUNE.

By HANNAH MORE.

May you fo raife your character that you may help to
make the next age a better thing, and leave pofterity
in your debt, for the advantage it fhall receive by your
example.　　　　　　　　LORD HALIFAX.

IN TWO VOLUMES.

VOL. I.

THE FIFTH EDITION.

LONDON:

PRINTED FOR T. CADELL JUN. AND W. DAVIES,
IN THE STRAND.
1799.

CONTENTS

OF THE

FIRST VOLUME.

———

VOL. I.   a   CHAP.

CHAP.

CHAP. XI.

CHAP. XII.

INTRODUCTION.

It is a singular injustice which is often exercised towards women, first to give them a very defective Education, and then to expect from them the most undeviating purity of conduct;—to train them in such a manner as shall lay them open to the most dangerous faults, and then to censure them for not proving faultless. Is it not unreasonable and unjust, to express disappointment if our daughters should, in their subsequent lives, turn out precisely that very kind of character for which it would be evident to an unprejudiced by-stander that the whole scope and tenor of their instruction had been systematically preparing them?

Some reflections on the present erroneous system are here with great deference submitted to public consideration. The

a 3   Author

More advocates for protecting women from corruption through education.

More inclined to change the "present erroneous system" in 1799 (Mansfield Park — 1814).

Author is apprehenfive that fhe fhall be accufed of betraying the interefts of her fex by laying open their defects: but furely, an earneft wifh to turn their attention to objects calculated to promote their true dignity, is not the office of an enemy. So to expofe the weaknefs of the land as to fuggeft the neceffity of internal improvement, and to point out the means of effectual defence, is not treachery, but patriotifm.

Again it may be objected to this little work, that many errors are here afcribed to women which by no means belong to them *exclufively*, and that it feems to confine to the fex thofe faults which are common to the fpecies: but this is in fome meafure unavoidable. In fpeaking on the qualities of one fex, the moralift is fomewhat in the fituation of the Geographer, who is treating on the nature of one country:—the air, foil, and produce of the land which he is defcribing, cannot fail in many effential points to refemble
thofe

Marginalia (handwritten):

Is this WORSE because it is coming from a woman?! FRIEDAN — Feminine Mystique is Concealed — women writers, etc.

thofe of other countries under the fame parallel; yet it is his bufinefs to defcant on the one without adverting to the other; and though in drawing his map he may happen to introduce fome of the neighbouring coaft, yet his principal attention muft be confined to that country which he propofes to defcribe, without taking into account the refembling circumftances of the adjacent fhores.

It may be alfo objected that the opinion here fuggefted on the ftate of manners among the higher claffes of our countrywomen, may feem to controvert the juft encomiums of modern travellers, who generally concur in afcribing a decided fuperiority to the ladies of this country over thofe of every other. But fuch is the ftate of foreign manners, that the comparative praife is almoft an injury to *Englifh* women. To be flattered for excelling thofe whofe ftandard of excellence is very low, is but a degrading kind of commendation; for the

value

value of all praife derived from fuperiority depends on the worth of the competitor. The character of Britifh ladies, with all the unparalleled advantages they poffefs, muft never be determined by a comparifon with the women of other nations, but by what they themfelves might be if all their talents and unrivalled opportunities were turned to the beft account.

Again, it may be faid, that the Author is lefs difpofed to expatiate on excellence than error: but the office of the hiftorian of human manners is delineation rather than panegyric. Were the end in view eulogium and not improvement, eulogium would have been far more gratifying, nor would juft objects for praife have been difficult to find. Even in her own limited fphere of obfervation, the Author is ac-quainted with much excellence in the clafs of which fhe treats;—with women who, poffeffing learning which would be thought extenfive in the other fex, fet an example of deep humility to their own;—
women

[handwritten marginal note:] It is the "beft account" that I am concerned with. The "beft account" fublimates identity (I argue) — creates a different kind of comptn.

women who, diſtinguiſhed for wit and genius, are eminent for domeſtic qualities ;—who, excelling in the fine arts, have carefully enriched their underſtandings ;—who, enjoying great affluence, devote it to the glory of God ;—who, poſſeſſing elevated rank, think their nobleſt ſtyle and title is that of a Chriſtian. *CHRISTIAN VALUES - enduring against corruption.*

That there is alſo much worth which is little known, ſhe is perſuaded; for it is the modeſt nature of goodneſs to exert itſelf quietly, while a few characters of the oppoſite caſt ſeem, by the rumour of their exploits, to fill the world; and by their noiſe to multiply their numbers. It often happens that a very ſmall party of people, by occuping the fore-ground, ſo ſeize the public attention, and monopolize the public talk, that *they* appear to be the great body : and a few active ſpirits, provided their activity take the wrong turn and ſupport the wrong cauſe, ſeem to fill the ſcene; and a few diſturbers of order, who have the talent of thus exciting a falſe

idea

idea of their multitudes by their mifchiefs,
actually gain ftrength and fwell their numbers by this fallacious arithmetic.

But the prefent work is no more intended
for a panegyric on thofe purer characters
who feek not human praife becaufe they act
from a higher motive, than for a fatire on
the avowedly licentious, who, urged by the
impulfe of the moment refift no inclination,
and, led away by the love of fafhion, diflike
no cenfure, fo it may ferve to refcue them
from neglect or oblivion.

There are, however, multitudes of the
young and the well-difpofed, who have as
yet taken no decided part, who are juft
launching on the ocean of life, juft about
to lofe their own right convictions, virtually preparing to counteract their better
propenfities, and unreluctantly yielding
themfelves to be carried down the tide of
popular practices, fanguine, thoughtlefs,
and confident of fafety.—To thefe the Author would gently hint, that, when once
embarked, it will be no longer eafy to fay

to

Corruption is caused by the passions - goes back to Plato. ^

to their paſſions, or even to their principles,
" Thus far ſhall ye go, and no further."
Their ſtruggles will grow fainter, their reſiſtance will become feebler, till borne down
by the confluence of example, temptation,
appetite, and habit, reſiſtance and oppoſition will ſoon be the only things of which
they will learn to be aſhamed.

e.g. Maria + Julia Bertram.

Should any reader revolt at what is
conceived to be unwarranted ſtrictneſs in
this little book, let it not be thrown by in
diſguſt before the following ſhort conſider-
ation be weighed.——If in this Chriſtian
country we are actually beginning to regard the ſolemn office of Baptiſm as
merely furniſhing an article to the pariſh
regiſter; — if we are learning from
our indefatigable Teachers, to conſider
this Chriſtian rite as a legal ceremony
retained for the ſole purpoſe of recording
the *age* of our children;—then, indeed,
the prevailing Syſtem of Education and
Manners on which theſe volumes preſume
to animadvert, may be adopted with propriety

priety and perfifted in with fafety, with
out entailing on our children or on ourfelves the peril of broken promifes or
the guilt of violated vows.——But, if the
obligation which Chriftian Baptifm impofes be really binding;—if the ordinance
have, indeed, a meaning beyond a mere
fecular tranfaction, beyond a record of
names and dates;—if it be an inftitution
by which the child is folemnly devoted to
God as his Father, to Jefus Chrift as his
Saviour, and to the Holy Spirit as his
Sanctifier; if there be no definite period
affigned when the obligation of fulfilling
the duties it enjoins fhall be fuperfeded;
—if, having once dedicated our offspring
to their Creator, we no longer dare to
mock Him by bringing them up in ignorance of His Will and neglect of His
Laws;—if, after having enlifted them.
under the banners of Chrift, to fight
manfully againft the three great enemies
of mankind, we are no longer at liberty
to let them lay down their arms; much
lefs

lefs to lead them to act as if they were in alliance inſtead of hoſtility with theſe ene-mies ;—if after having promiſed that they ſhall renounce the vanities of the world, we are not allowed to invalidate the engage-ment ;—if after ſuch a covenant we ſhould tremble to make theſe renounced vanities the ſupreme object of our own purſuit or of *their* inſtruction ;—if all this be really ſo, then the Strictures on Modern Educa-tion in the firſt of theſe Volumes, and on the Habits of poliſhed Life in the ſecond, will not be found ſo repugnant to truth, and reaſon, and common ſenſe, as may on a firſt view be ſuppoſed.

But if on candidly ſumming up the evi-dence, the deſign and ſcope of the Author be fairly judged, not by the cuſtoms or opinions of the worldly, (for every Engliſh ſubject has a right to object to a ſuſpected or prejudiced jury,) but by an appeal to that divine law which is the only infallible rule of judgment ; if on ſuch an appeal her views and principles ſhall be found cenſur-able

able for their rigour, abſurd in their re-
quiſitions, or prepoſterous in their reſtric-
tions, ſhe will have no right to complain of
ſuch a verdict, becauſe ſhe will then ſtand
condemned by that court to whoſe deciſion
ſhe implicitly ſubmits.

Let it not be ſuſpected that the Author
arrogantly conceives herſelf to be exempt
from that natural corruption of the heart
which it is one chief object of this ſlight
work to exhibit; that ſhe ſuperciliouſly
erects herſelf into the impeccable cenſor of
her ſex and of the world; as if from the
critic's chair ſhe were coldly pointing out
the faults and errors of another order of
beings, in whoſe welfare ſhe had not that
lively intereſt which can only flow from the
tender and intimate participation of fellow-
feeling.

With a deep ſelf-abaſement ariſing from
a ſtrong conviction of being indeed a par-
taker in the ſame corrupt nature; together
with a full perſuaſion of the many and great
defects of theſe Volumes, and a ſincere con-
ſciouſneſs

ícioufnefs of her inability to do juftice to a
fubject which, however, a fenfe of duty ✳
impelled her to undertake, fhe commits
herfelf to the candour of that Public which
has fo frequently, in her inftance, accepted
a right intention as a fubftitute for a powerful performance.

BATH,
March 14, 1799.

STRICTURES

STRICTURES

ON THE

MODERN SYSTEM

OF

FEMALE EDUCATION.

CHAP. I.

k Important —
Contextualise.

*Addreſs to women of rank and fortune, on
the effects of their influence on ſociety.—
Suggeſtions for the exertion of it in various
inſtances.*

Among the talents for the application of
which women of the higher claſs will
be peculiarly accountable, there is one,
the importance of which they can ſcarcely
rate too highly. This talent is influence.
We read of the greateſt orator of antiquity,
that the wiſeſt plans which it had coſt him
years to frame, a woman could overturn

VOL. I.   B   in

in a fingle day ; and when one confiders
the variety of mifchiefs which an ill-
directed influence has been known to produce, one is led to reflect with the moft
fanguine hope on the beneficial effects to
be expected from the fame powerful force
when exerted in its true direction.

The general ftate of civilized fociety
depends more than thofe are aware who
are not accuftomed to fcrutinize into the
fprings of human action, on the prevailing
fentiments and habits of women, and
on the nature and degree of the eftimation
in which they are held. Even thofe who
admit the power of female elegance on
the manners of men, do not always attend
to the influence of female principles on
their character. In the former cafe, indeed, women are apt to be fufficiently
confcious of their power, and not backward in turning it to account. But there
are nobler objects to be effected by the
exertion of their powers, and unfortunately, ladies, who are often unreafonably
confident where they ought to be diffident,

are

are fometimes capricioufly diffident juft
when they ought to feel where their true
importance lies ; and feeling, to exert it.
To ufe their boafted power over mankind
to no higher purpofe than the gratification
of vanity or the indulgence of pleafure, is
the degrading triumph of thofe fair victims
to luxury, caprice, and defpotifm, whom
the laws and the religion of the voluptuous
prophet of Arabia exclude from light, and
liberty, and knowledge; and it is humbling
to reflect, that in thofe countries in which
fondnefs for the mere perfons of women is
carried to the higheft excefs, *they are
flaves ;* and that their moral and intellectual degradation increafes in direct proportion to the adoration which is paid to
mere external charms.

But I turn to the bright reverfe of this
mortifying fcene ; to a country where our
fex enjoys the bleffings of liberal inftruction, of reafonable laws, of a pure
religion, and all the endearing pleafures of an equal, focial, virtuous, and
delightful intercourfe : I turn with an

earneft

earneſt hope, that women, thus richly en-
dowed with the bounties of Providence,
will not content themſelves with poliſhing,
when they are able to reform; with entertaining, when they may awaken; and with
captivating for a day, when they may bring
into action powers of which the effects may
be commenſurate with eternity.

In this moment of alarm and peril,
I would call on them with a " warning
" voice," which ſhould ſtir up every
latent principle in their minds, and kindle
every ſlumbering energy in their hearts;
I would call on them to come forward,
and contribute their full and fair proportion towards the ſaving of their country.
But I would call on them to come forward,
without departing from the refinement of
their character, without derogating from
the dignity of their rank, without blemiſh-
ing the delicacy of their ſex : I would
call them to the beſt and moſt appropriate
exertion of their power, to raiſe the de-
preſſed tone of public morals, and to
awaken the drowſy ſpirit of religious principle.

ciple. They know too well how arbitrarily they give the law to manners, and with how defpotic a fway they fix the ftandard of fafhion. But this is not enough; this is a low mark, a prize not worthy of their high and holy calling. For, on the ufe which women of the fuperior clafs may now be difpofed to make of that power delegated to them by the courtefy of cuftom, by the honeft gallantry of the heart, by the imperious control of virtuous affections, by the habits of civilized ftates, by the ufages of polifhed fociety; on the ufe, I fay, which they fhall hereafter make of this influence, will depend, in no low degree, the well-being of thofe ftates, and the virtue and happinefs, nay perhaps the very exiftence, of that fociety. (upper class society).

At this period, when our country can only hope to ftand by oppofing a bold and noble *unanimity* to the moft tremendous confederacies againft religion, and order, and governments, which the world ever ſaw; what an acceſſion would it bring to the public ſtrength, could we prevail on beauty, and rank, and talents, and virtue, confederating their ſeveral powers, to come forward with a patriotiſm at once firm and feminine, for the general good! I am not founding an alarm to female warriors, or exciting female politicians: I hardly know which of the two is the moſt diſguſting and unnatural character. Propriety is to a woman what the great Roman critic ſays action is to an orator; it is the firſt, the ſecond, the third requiſite. A woman may be knowing, active, witty, and amuſing; but without propriety ſhe cannot be amiable. Propriety is the centre in which all the lines of duty and of agreeableneſs meet. It is to character what proportion is to figure, and grace to attitude. It does not depend on any one perfection, but it is the reſult of general excellence. It ſhews itſelf by a regular, orderly, undeviating courſe; and never ſtarts from its ſober orbit into any ſplendid eccentricities; for

it

!!!

women must be repressed to be dignified.

(repressed)

Propriety = conformity to conventionally acceptable standards of behaviour.

it would be afhamed of fuch praife as
it might extort by any aberrations from
its proper path. It renounces all commendation but what is characteriftic ; and
I would make it the criterion of true
tafte, right principle, and genuine feeling,
in a woman, whether fhe would be lefs
touched with all the flattery of romantic
and exaggerated panegyric than with that
beautiful picture of correct and elegant
propriety, which Milton draws of our firft
mother, when he delineates

" Thofe thoufand *decencies* which daily flow
" From all her words and actions."

Even the influence of religion is to be
exercifed with difcretion. A female Po-
lemic wanders nearly as far from the
limits prefcribed to her fex, as a female
Machiavel or warlike Thaleftris. Fierce-
nefs has made almoft as few converts as the
fword, and both are peculiarly ungraceful
in a female. Even *religious* violence has
human tempers of its own to indulge,

and

and is gratifying itſelf when it would be thought to be ſerving God. Let not the bigot place her natural paſſions to the account of Chriſtianity, or imagine ſhe is pious when ſhe is only paſſionate. Let her bear in mind that a Chriſtian doctrine is always to be defended with a Chriſtian ſpirit, and not make herſelf amends by the ſtoutneſs of her orthodoxy for the badneſs of her temper. Many, becauſe they defend a religious opinion with pertinacity, ſeem to fancy that they thereby acquire a kind of right to withhold the obedience which ſhould be neceſſarily involved in the principle.

No Paſſions.

But the character of a conſiſtent Chriſtian is as carefully to be maintained, as that of a fiery diſputant is to be avoided ; and ſhe who is afraid to avow her principles, or aſhamed to defend them, has little claim to that honourable title. A profligate, who laughs at the moſt ſacred inſtitutions, and keeps out of the way of every thing which comes under the appearance of formal inſtruction, may be diſconcerted

concerted by the modeſt, but ſpirited re-
buke of a delicate woman, whoſe life
adorns the doctrines which her conver-
ſation defends: but ſhe who adminiſters
reproof with ill-breeding, defeats the effect
of her remedy. On the other hand, there
is a diſhoneſt way of labouring to con-
ciliate the favour of a whole company,
though of characters and principles irre-
concilably oppoſite. The words may be
ſo guarded as not to ſhock the believer,
while the eye and voice may be ſo accom-
modated, as not to diſcourage the infidel.
She who, with a half earneſtneſs, trims
between the truth and the faſhion; who,
while ſhe thinks it creditable to defend the
cauſe of religion, yet does it in a faint
tone, a ſtudied ambiguity of phraſe, and a
certain expreſſion in her countenance,
which proves that ſhe is not diſpleaſed
with what ſhe affects to cenſure, or that
ſhe is afraid to loſe her reputation for
wit, in proportion as ſhe advances her
credit for piety, injures the cauſe more
than

than he who attacked it; for fhe proves, either that fhe does not believe what fhe profeffes, or that fhe does not reverence what fear compels her to believe. But this is not all: fhe is called on, not barely to reprefs impiety, but to excite, to encourage, and to cherifh every tendency to ferious religion.

Some of the occafions of contributing to the general good which are daily prefenting themfelves to ladies, are almoft too minute to be pointed out. Yet of the good which right-minded women, anxioufly watching thefe minute occafions, and adroitly feizing them, might accomplifh, we may form fome idea by the ill-effects which we actually fee produced, through the mere levity, carelefnefs, and inattention (to fay no worfe) of fome of thofe ladies, who are looked up to as ftandards in the fafhionable world.

I am perfuaded, if many a one, who is now diffeminating unintended mifchief, under the dangerous notion that there

is

is no harm in any thing fhort of pofitive vice, and under the falfe colours of that indolent humility, "What good can *I* " do?" could be brought to fee in *its* collected force the annual aggregate of the random evil fhe is daily doing, by conftantly throwing a *little* cafual weight into the wrong fcale, by mere inconfiderate and unguarded chat, fhe would ftart from her felf-complacent dream. If fhe could conceive how much fhe may be diminifhing the good impreffions of *young* men; and if fhe could imagine how little amiable levity or irreligion makes her appear in the eyes of thofe who are older and abler, (however loofe their own principles may be,) fhe would correct herfelf in the firft inftance, from pure good nature; and in the fecond, from worldly prudence and mere felf-love. But on how much higher principles would fhe reftrain herfelf, if fhe habitually took into account the important doctrine of confequences: and if fhe reflected that the

lefier

leſſer but more habitual corruptions make up by their number, what they may ſeem to come ſhort of by their weight: then perhaps ſhe would find that, among the higher claſs of women, *inconſideration* is adding more to the daily quantity of evil than almoſt all other cauſes put together.

There is an inſtrument of inconceivable force, when it is employed againſt the intereſts of Chriſtianity. It is not reaſoning, for that may be anſwered; it is not learning, for luckily the infidel is not ſeldom ignorant; it is not invective, for we leave ſo coarſe an engine to the hands of the vulgar; it is not evidence, for happily we have that on our ſide: it is RIDICULE, the moſt deadly weapon in the whole arſenal of impiety, and which becomes an almoſt unerring ſhaft when directed by a fair and faſhionable hand. No maxim has been more readily adopted, or is more intrinſically falſe, than that which the faſcinating eloquence of a noble ſceptic of the

the laſt age contrived to render ſo popular, that " ridicule is the teſt of truth." It is no teſt of truth itſelf; but of their firm-neſs who aſſert the cauſe of truth, it is in-deed a ſevere teſt. This light, keen, miſ-ſile weapon, the irreſolute, unconfirmed Chriſtian will find it harder to withſtand, than the whole heavy artillery of infidelity united.

A young man of the better ſort, having juſt entered upon the world, with a certain ſhare of good diſpoſitions and right feel-ings, not ignorant of the evidences, nor deſtitute of the principles of Chriſtianity; without parting with his reſpect for re-ligion, he ſets out with the too natural wiſh of making himſelf a reputation, and of ſtanding well with the faſhionable part of the female world. He preſerves for a time a horror of vice, which makes it not difficult for him to reſiſt the groſſer cor-ruptions of ſociety; he can as yet repel profaneneſs; nay, he can withſtand the banter of a club. He has ſenſe enough to

ſee

fee through the miferable fallacies of the
new philofophy, and fpirit enough to
expofe its malignity. So far he does
well, and you are ready to congratulate
him on his fecurity. You are miftaken:
the principles of the ardent, and hitherto
promifing adventurer are fhaken, juft in
that very fociety where, while he was
looking for pleafure, he doubted not of
fafety. In the company of certain women
of good fafhion and no ill fame, he makes
fhipwreck of his religion. He fees them
treat with levity or derifion fubjects which
he has been ufed to hear named with
refpect. He could confute an argument,
he could unravel a fophiftry; but he
cannot ftand a laugh. A fneer, not at
the truth of religion, for that perhaps is by
none of the party difbelieved, but at its
gravity, its unfeafonablenefs, its dulnefs,
puts all his refolution to flight. He feels his
miftake, and ftruggles to recover his credit;
in order to which, he adopts the gay affectation of trying to feem worfe than he

(They ridicule his religion).

really

really is, he goes on to fay things which
he does not believe, and to deny things
which he does believe, and all to efface
the firft impreffion, and to recover a reputation which he has committed to *their*
hands on whofe report he knows he
fhall ftand or fall, in thofe circles in which
he is ambitious to fhine.

That cold compound of irony, irreligion,
felfifhnefs, and fneer, which make up
what the French (from whom we borrow
the thing as well as the word) fo well
exprefs by the term *perfiflage*, has of
late years made an incredible progrefs
in blafting the opening buds of piety in
young perfons of fafhion. A cold plea-
fantry, a temporary cant word, the jargon
of the day (for the " great vulgar" have
their jargon) blights the firft promife of
ferioufnefs. The ladies of *ton* have certain watch-words, which may be detected
as indications of this fpirit. The clergy
are fpoken of under the contemptuous appellation of *The Parfons*. Some ludicrous
affociation

affociation is infallibly combined with every idea of religion. If a warm hearted youth has ventured to name with enthufiafm fome eminently pious character, his glowing ardour is extinguifhed with a laugh; and a drawling declaration, that the perfon in queftion is really a mighty *harmlefs* good creature, is uttered in a tone which leads the youth fecretly to vow, that whatever elfe he may be, he will never be a good harmlefs creature.

Nor is ridicule more dangerous to true piety than to true tafte. An age which values itfelf on parody, burlefque, irony, and caricature, produces little that is fublime, either in genius or in virtue; but they *amufe*, and we live in an age which *muft* be amufed, though genius, feeling, truth, and principle, be the facrifice. Nothing chills the ardours of devotion like a frigid farcafm; and, in the feafon of youth, the mind fhould be kept particularly clear of all light affociations. This is of fo much importance, that I

have

young people must not let their minds become corrupt.

have known perfons who, having been early accuftomed to certain ludicrous combinations, were never able to get their minds cleanfed from the impurities contracted by this habitual levity, even after a thorough reformation in their hearts and lives had taken place : their principles became reformed, but their imaginations were indelibly foiled. They could defift from fins which the ftrictnefs of Chriftianity would not allow them to commit, but they could not difmifs from their minds images, which her purity forbade them to entertain.

There was a time when a variety of epithets were 'thought neceffary to exprefs various kinds of excellence, and when the different qualities of the mind were diftinguifhed by appropriate and difcriminating terms ; when the words venerable, learned, fagacious, profound, acute, pious, worthy, ingenious, valuable, elegant, agreeable, wife, or witty, were ufed as fpecific marks of diftinct characters. But the legiflators of fashion have of late years thought proper to comprise all merit in one established epithet, and it must be confessed to be a very desirable one as far as it goes. This epithet is exclusively and indiscriminately applied wherever commendation is intended. The word *pleasant* now serves to combine and express all moral and intellectual excellence. Every individual, from the gravest professors of the gravest profession, down to the trifler who is of no profession at all, must earn the epithet of *pleasant*, or must be contented to be nothing; and must be consigned over to ridicule, under the vulgar and inexpressive cant word of a *bore*. This is the mortifying designation of many a respectable man, who, though of much worth and much ability, cannot perhaps clearly make out his letters patent to the title of *pleasant*. For, according to this modern classification, there is no intermediate state, but all are comprised within the ample bounds of one or other of these two terms.

We ought to be more on our guard againſt this ſpirit of ridicule, becauſe, whatever may be the character of the preſent day, its faults do not ſpring from the redundancies of great qualities, or the overflowings of extravagant virtues. It is well if more correct views of life, a more regular adminiſtration of laws, and a more ſettled ſtate of ſociety, have helped to reſtrain the exceſſes of the heroic ages, when love and war were conſidered as the great and ſole buſineſs of human life. Yet, if that period was marked by a romantic extravagance, and the preſent by an indolent ſelfiſhneſs, our ſuperiority is not ſo triumphantly deciſive, as, in the vanity of our hearts, we may be ready to imagine.

I do not wiſh to bring back the frantic reign of chivalry, nor to reinſtate women in that fantaſtic empire in which they then ſat enthroned in the hearts, or rather in the imaginations of men. Common ſenſe is an excellent material of univerſal application,

c 2

application, which the fagacity of latter
ages has feized upon, and rationally
applied to the bufinefs of common life.
But let us not forget, in the infolence
of acknowledged fuperiority, that it was
religion and chaftity, operating on the
romantic fpirit of thofe times, which eftablifhed the defpotic fway of woman; and
though fhe now no longer looks down
on her adoring votaries, from the pedeftal
to which an abfurd idolatry had lifted
her, yet let her remember that it is the
fame religion and the fame chaftity which
once raifed her to fuch an elevation, that
muft ftill furnifh the nobleft energies of her
character.

While we lawfully ridicule the abfurdities which we have abandoned, let us
not plume ourfelves on that fpirit of
novelty which glories in the oppofite ex-
treme. If the manners of the period
in queftion were affected, and if the gallantry was unnatural, yet the tone of
virtue was high; and let us remember
that

that conftancy, purity, and honour, are not ridiculous in themfelves, though they may unluckily be affociated with qualities which are fo: and women of delicacy would do well to reflect, when defcanting on thofe exploded manners, how far it be decorous to deride with too broad a laugh, attachments which could fubfift on remote gratifications; or grofsly to ridicule the tafte which led the admirer to facrifice pleafure to refpect, and inclination to honour; to fneer at that purity which made felf-denial a proof of affection, and to call in queftion the found underftanding of him who preferred the fame of his miftrefs to his own indulgence.

One cannot but be ftruck with the wonderful contraft exhibited to our view, when we contemplate the manners of the two periods in queftion. In the former, all the flower of Europe fmit with a delirious gallantry; all that was young, and noble, and brave, and great, with a fanatic frenzy and prepofterous con-

c 3   tempt

tempt of danger, traverſed ſeas, and ſcaled
mountains, and compaſſed a large portion
of the globe, at the expence of eaſe, and
fortune, and life, for the unprofitable project of reſcuing, by force of arms, from the
hands of infidels, the ſepulchre of that Saviour, whom, *in the other period*, their
poſterity would think it the height of fa-
naticiſm ſo much as to name in good company: whoſe altars they deſert, whoſe
temples they neglect; and though in more
than one country at leaſt they ſtill call
themſelves by his name, yet too many, it
is to be feared, contemn his precepts, ſtill
more are aſhamed of his doctrines, and
not a few reject his ſacrifice. Too many
confider Chriſtianity rather as a political
than a religious diſtinction; too many
claim the appellation of Chriſtians, in mere
oppoſition to that Democracy with which
they conceive infidelity to be aſſociated,
rather than from an abhorrence of impiety
for its own ſake; and dread irreligion as
the ſuppoſed badge of a reprobated party,

more

more than on account of that moral corruption which is its inseparable concomitant.

On the other hand, in an age when inversion is the order of the day, the modern idea of improvement does not consist in altering, but extirpating. We do not reform, but subvert. We do not correct old systems, but demolish them; fancying that when every thing shall be new it will be perfect. Not to have been wrong, but to have been at all, is the crime. Excellence is no longer considered as an experimental thing which is to grow gradually out of observation and practice, and to be improved by the accumulating additions brought by the wisdom of successive ages. *Our wisdom* is not slowly brought by age and gradual growth to perfection, but is a goddess which starts at once, full grown, mature, armed cap-à-pee, from the heads of our modern thunderers. Or rather, if I may change the allusion, a perfect system is *now* expected inevitably to spring at once, like the fabled bird of Arabia, from the ashes of its parent; and, like that, can re-

ceive

ceive its birth no other way but by the deftruction of its predeceffor.

Inftead of clearing away what is re-
dundant, pruning what is cumberfome,
fupplying what is defective, and amending
what is wrong, we adopt the indefinite
rage for radical reform of Jack, who
in altering Lord Peter's * coat, fhewed his
zeal by crying out, " Tear away, brother
" Martin, for the love of heaven ; never
" mind, fo you do but tear away."

This tearing fyftem has unqueftionably
rent away fome valuable parts of that
ftrong, rich, native ftuff, which formed the
ancient texture of Britifh manners. That
we have gained much I am perfuaded ;
that we have loft nothing I dare not therefore affirm. But though it fairly exhibits a mark of our improved judgment
to ridicule the fantaftic notions of love and
honour in the heroic ages ; let us not
rejoice that that fpirit of generofity in
fentiment, and of ardour in piety, the

---

* Swift's " Tale of a Tub."

exu-

i.e.) let us not rejoice that piety + refinement are now 'old'.

exuberancies of which were then fo inconvenient, are now funk as unreafonably low. That revolution of manners which the unparalleled wit and genius of Don Quixote fo happily effected, by abolifhing extravagancies the moft abfurd and pernicious, was fo far imperfect, that fome virtues which he never meant to expofe, fell into difrepute with the abfurdities which he did: and it is become the turn of the prefent tafte to attach in no fmall degree that which is ridiculous to that which is ferious and heroic. Some modern works of wit have affifted in bringing piety and fome of the nobleft virtues into contempt, by ftudioufly affociating them with oddity, childifh fimplicity, and ignorance of the world: and unneceffary pains have been taken to extinguifh that zeal and ardour, which, however liable to excefs and error, are yet the fpring of whatever is great and excellent in the human character. The novel of Cervantes is incomparable; the Tartuffe of Moliere is unequalled; but

true

→ God-creator versus Darwin, Science. (1859; later).

true generofity and true religion will never lofe any thing of their intrinfic value, becaufe knight-errantry and hypocrify are legitimate objects for fatire.

But to return from this too long digreffion, to the fubject of female influence. Thofe who have not watched the united operation of vanity and feeling on a youthful mind, will not conceive how much lefs formidable the ridicule of all his own fex will be to a very young man, than that of thofe women to whom he has been taught to look up as the arbitreffes of elegance. Such an one, I doubt not, might be able to work himfelf up, by the force of genuine chriftian principles, to fuch a pitch of true heroifm, as to refufe a challenge, (and it requires more real courage to refufe a challenge than to accept one,) who would yet be in danger of relapfing into the dreadful pufillanimity of the world, when he is told that no woman of fafhion will hereafter look on him but with contempt. While we have cleared

away

away the rubbifh of the Gothic ages, it
were to be wifhed we had not retained the
moft criminal of all their inftitutions.
While chivalry fhould indicate a madman,
while its leading object, the *fingle combat*,
fhould defignate a gentleman, has not yet
been explained. Nay the original motive
is loft, while the finful practice is continued; for the fighter of the duel no
longer *pretends* to be a glorious redreffer
of the wrongs of ftrangers; no longer confiders himfe as pioufly appealing to heaven for the juftice of his caufe; but
from the flavifh fear of unmerited reproach, often felfifhly hazards the happinefs of his neareft connections, and always
comes forth in direct defiance of an
acknowledged command of the Almighty.
Perhaps there are few occafions in which
female influence might be exerted to a
higher purpofe than in this, in which laws
and confcience have hitherto effected fo
little. But while the duellift (who perhaps becomes a duellift only becaufe he
was

was firſt a ſeducer) is welcomed with
ſmiles; the more hardy youth, who, not
becaufe he fears man but God, declines
a challenge; who is refolved to brave
difgrace rather than commit fin, would be
treated with cool contempt by thofe very
perfons to whofe efteem he might reafonably look, as one of the rewards of his
true and fubftantial fortitude.

How then is it to be reconciled with the
decifions of principle, that delicate women
fhould receive with complacency the fuccefsful libertine, who has been detected by
the wretched father or the injured hufband
in a criminal commerce, the difcovery of
which has too juftly banifhed the unhappy
partner of his crime from virtuous fociety?
Nay, if he happen to be very handfome, or
very brave, or very fafhionable, is there
not fometimes a kind of difhonourable
competition for his favour? But, whether
his popularity be derived from birth, or
parts, or perfon, or (what is often a fubftitute for all) from his having made
his

his way into *good company*, women of diftinction fully the fanctity of virtue by the too vifible pleafure they fometimes exprefs at the attentions of fuch a popular libertine, whofe voluble fmall-talk they admire, and whofe fprightly nothings they quote, and whom perhaps their very favour tends to prevent from becoming a better character, becaufe he finds himfelf more acceptable as he is.

May I be allowed to introduce a new part of my fubject, by remarking that it is a matter of inconceivable importance, though not perhaps fufficiently confidered, when any popular work, not on a religious topic, but on any common fubject, fuch as politics, hiftory, or fcience, has happened to be written by an author of found Chriftian principles? It may not have been neceffary, nor prudently practicable, to have a fingle page in the whole work profeffedly religious: but ftill, when the living principle informs the mind of the writer, it is almoft impoffible but that fomething of its fpirit will

2 diffufe

diffuſe itſelf even into ſubjects with which
it ſhould ſeem but remotely connected.
It is at leaſt a comfort to the reader,
to feel that honeſt confidence which reſults
from knowing that he has put himſelf into
ſafe hands; that he has committed himſelf
to an author, whoſe known principles are
a pledge that his reader need not be
driven to watch himſelf at every ſtep with
anxious circumſpection; that he need not
be looking on the right hand and on
the left, as if he knew they were pitfalls
under the flowers which are delighting him.
And it is no ſmall point gained, that on
ſubjects in which you do not look to
improve your religion, it is at leaſt ſecured
from deterioration. If the Athenian laws
were ſo delicate that they diſgraced any one
who ſhewed an inquiring traveller the
wrong road, what diſgrace, among Chriſtians, ſhould attach to that author, who,
when a youth is inquiring the road to
hiſtory or philoſophy, directs him to blaſ-
phemy and unbelief?

In

In animadverting farther on the reigning evils which the times more particularly demand that women of rank and influence should reprefs, Chriftianity calls upon them to bear their decided teftimony againft every thing which is notorioufly contributing to the public corruption. It calls upon them to banifh from their dreffing-rooms, (and oh, that their influence could banifh from the libraries of their fons and hufbands!) that fober and unfufpected mafs of mifchief, which, by affuming the plaufible names of Science, of Philofophy, of Arts, of Belles Lettres, is gradually adminiftering death to the principles of thofe who would be on their guard, had the poifon been labelled with its own pernicious title. Avowed attacks upon revelation are more eafily refifted, becaufe the malignity is advertifed. But who fufpects the deftruction which lurks under the harmlefs or inftructive names of *General Hiftory, Natural Hiftory, Travels, Voyages, Lives, Encyclopedias, Criticifm, and Romance?*

mance? Who will deny that many of thefe works contain much admirable matter; brilliant paffages, important facts, juft defcriptions, faithful pictures of nature, and valuable illuftrations of fcience? But while " the dead fly lies at the bottom," the whole will exhale a corrupt and peftilential ftench. *the deeper meaning?*

Novels, which chiefly ufed to be dangerous in one refpect, are now become mifchievous in a thoufand. They are continually fhifting their ground, and enlarging their fphere, and are daily becoming vehicles of wider mifchief. Sometimes they concentrate their force, and are at once employed to diffufe deftructive politics, deplorable profligacy, and impudent infidelity. Roufleau was the firft popular difpenfer of this complicated drug, in which the deleterious infufion was ftrong, and the effect proportionably fatal. For he does not attempt to feduce the affections but through the medium of the principles. He does not paint an innocent

woman,

woman, ruined, repenting, and reftored; but with a far more mifchievous refine-ment, he annihilates the value of chaftity, and with pernicious fubtlety attempts to make his heroine appear almoft more ami-able without it. He exhibits a virtuous woman, the victim not of temptation but of reafon, not of vice but of fentiment, not of paffion but of conviction; and ftrikes at the very root of honour by elevating a crime into a principle. With a metaphyfical fophiftry the moft plaufible, he debauches the heart of woman, by che-rifhing her vanity in the erection of a fyf-tem of male virtues, to which, with a lofty dereliction of thofe that are her more pecu-liar and characteriftic praife, he tempts her to afpire; powerfully infinuating, that to this fplendid fyftem chaftity does not necef-farily belong: thus corrupting the judg-ment and bewildering the underftanding, as the moft effectual way to inflame the imagination and deprave the heart.

The

The rare mifchief of this author confifts
in his power of feducing by falfehood
thofe who love truth, but whofe minds are
ftill wavering, and whofe principles are
not yet formed. He allures the warm-
hearted to embrace vice; not becaufe they
prefer vice, but becaufe he gives to vice fo
natural an air of virtue : and ardent and
enthufiaftic youth, too confidently trufting
in their integrity and in their teacher, will
be undone, while they fancy they are indulging in the nobleft feelings of their
nature. Many authors will more infallibly
complete the ruin of the loofe and ill-
difpofed : but perhaps (if I may change
the figure) there never was a net of fuch
exquifite art and inextricable workman-
fhip, fpread to entangle innocence and
enfnare inexperience, as the writings of
Rouffeau : and, unhappily, the victim does
not even ftruggle in the toils, becaufe part
of the delufion confrfts in imagining that
he is fet at liberty.

Some

Some of our recent popular publications
have adopted and enlarged all the mifchiefs
of this fchool, and the principal evil arifing
from them is, that the virtues they exhibit
are almoft more dangerous than the vices.
The chief materials out of which thefe
delufive fyftems are framed, are characters
who practife fuperfluous acts of generofity,
while they are trampling on obvious and
commanded duties ; who combine inflated
fentiments of honour with actions the moft
flagitious ; a high tone of felf-confidence,
with a perpetual neglect of felf-denial : pa-
thetic apoftrophes to the paffions, but no attempt to refift them. They teach, that chaftity is only individual attachment ; that no
duty exifts which is not prompted by feeling ; that impulfe is the main fpring of *
virtuous actions, while laws and religion
are only unjuft reftraints ; the former im-   *(reftrains)*
pofed by arbitrary men, the latter by the
abfurd prejudices of timorous and un-
enlightened confcience. Alas ! they do
not know that the beft creature of impulfe

D 2   that

that ever lived is but a wayward, unfixed
unprincipled being! that the beſt *natural*
man requires a curb; and needs that balance to the affections which Chriſtianity
alone can furniſh, and without which benevolent propenſities are no ſecurity to virtue.
And perhaps it is not too much to ſay, in
ſpite of the monopoly of benevolence to
which the new philoſophy lays claim, that
the *human* duties of the ſecond table have
never once been well performed by any of
the rejectors of that previous portion of the
Decalogue which enjoins duty to *God*.

In ſome of the moſt ſplendid of theſe characters compaſſion is erected into the throne
of juſtice, and juſtice degraded into the
rank of plebeian virtues. Creditors are
defrauded, while the money due to them
is laviſhed in dazzling acts of charity
to ſome object that affects the ſenſes;
which fits of charity are made the ſponge
cf every ſin, and the ſubſtitute of every
virtue: the whole indirectly tending to
intimate how very *benevolent people are who*

are

are not Christians. From many of these compositions, indeed, Christianity is systematically, and always virtually, excluded; for the law, and the prophets, and the gospel *can* make no part of a scheme in which this world is looked upon as all in all ; in which want and misery are considered as evils arising solely from human governments, and not from the dispensations of God ; in which poverty is represented as merely a political evil, and the restraints which tend to keep the poor honest, are painted as the most flagrant injustice. The gospel *can* make no part of a system in which the chimerical project of consummate earthly happiness (founded on the mad pretence of loving the poor better than God loves them) would defeat the divine plan, which meant this world a scene of discipline, not of remuneration. The gospel *can* have nothing to do with a system in which sin is reduced to a little human imperfection, and Old Bailey crimes are softened down into a few engaging

D 3   weak-

[Handwritten marginalia, top:] & This is More's main concern — modern education system encourages women to "reason" and to read sciences, etc.

[Handwritten marginalia, right:] It neglects Christian Values; More attempts to address / amend.

weaknesses; and in which the turpitude of all the vices a man himself commits, is done away by his *candour* in tolerating all the vices committed by others.

But the part of the system the most fatal to that class whom I am addressing is, that even in those works which do not go all the length of treating marriage as an unjust infringement on liberty, and a tyrannical deduction from general happiness; yet it commonly happens that the hero or heroine, who has practically violated the letter of the seventh commandment, and continues to live in the allowed violation of its spirit, is painted as so amiable and so benevolent, so tender or so brave; and the temptation is represented as so *irresistible*, (for all these philosophers are fatalists,) the predominant and cherished sin is so filtered and defecated of its pollutions, and is so sheltered and surrounded, and relieved with shining qualities, that the innocent and impressible young reader is brought to lose all horror of the

I   awful

[right margin, handwritten:] ADULTERY   7

[left margin, handwritten:] E.g. M+J in Mansfield Park.

[bottom, handwritten:] Novels corrupting the reader —
E.G. The play in Mansfield Park !!!
FANNY's REFUSAL!

awful crime in queſtion, in the compla
cency ſhe feels for the engaging virtues of
the criminal.

But there is another object to which I
would direct the exertion of that power
of female influence of which I am ſpeaking.
Thoſe ladies who take the lead in ſociety
are loudly called upon to act as the
guardians of the public taſte as well as
of the public virtue. They are called
upon, therefore, to oppoſe with the whole
weight of their influence, the irruption
of thoſe ſwarms of publications now
daily iſſuing from the banks of the
Danube, which, like their ravaging predeceſſors of the darker ages, though with
far other arms, are overrunning civilized
ſociety. Thoſe readers, whoſe purer taſte
has been formed on the correct models
of the old claſſic ſchool, ſee with indignation and aſtoniſhment the Huns and Van-
dals once more overpowering the Greeks,
and Romans. They behold our minds,
with a retrograde but rapid motion, hurried

back

back to the reign of " chaos and old
" night," by diſtorted and unprincipled
compoſitions, which unite the taſte of the
Goths with the morals of Bagſhot *,

Gorgons, and Hydras, and Chimeras dire !

They terrify the weak, and diſguſt the
diſcerning, by wild and mis-ſhapen ſuperſti-
tions, in which, with that *conſiſtency* which
forms ſo ſtriking a feature of the new philoſophy, thoſe who moſt earneſtly deny the
immortality of the ſoul are moſt eager to
introduce the machinery of ghoſts.

The writings of the French infidels were
ſome years ago circulated in England with
uncommon induſtry and with ſome effect :
but the plain ſenſe and good principles
of the far greater part of our countrymen
reſiſted the attack, and roſe ſuperior to the
trial. Of the doctrines and principles here
alluded to, the dreadful conſequences, not

* The newſpapers announce that Schiller's Tragedy
of the Robbers, which inflamed the young nobility
of Germany to inliſt themſelves into a band of
highwaymen to rob in the foreſts of Bohemia, is
now acting in England by perſons of quality!

only

only in the unhappy country where they
originated and were almoſt univerſally
adopted, but in every part of Europe
where they have been received, have been
ſuch as to ſerve as a beacon to ſurrounding
nations, if any warning can preſerve them
from deſtruction. In this country the
ſubject is now ſo well underſtood, that
every thing that iſſues from the *French*
preſs is received with jealouſy; and a work,
on the firſt appearance of its exhibiting the
doctrines of Voltaire and his aſſociates, is
rejected with indignation.

But let us not on account of this
victory repoſe in confident ſecurity. The
modern apoſtles of infidelity and im-
morality, little leſs indefatigable in dif-
perſing their pernicious doctrines than the
firſt apoſtles were in propagating goſpel
truths, have indeed changed their weapons,
but they have by no means deſiſted from
the attack. To deſtroy the principles of
Chriſtianity in this iſland, appears at the
preſent moment to be their grand aim.
Oeprived of the aſſiſtance of the French
preſs,

prefs, they are now attempting to attain their object under the clofe and more artificial veil of German literature. Confcious that religion and morals will ftand or fall together, their attacks are fometimes levelled againft the one, and fometimes againft the other. With ftrong occafional profeffions of general attachment to both of thefe, they endeavour to intereft the feelings of the reader, fometimes in favour of fome one particular vice, at other times on the fubject of fome one objection to revealed religion. Poetry as well as profe, romance as well as hiftory, writings on philofophical as well as on political fubjects, have thus been employed to inftil the principles of *Illuminatifm*, while incredible pains have been taken to obtain able tranflations of every book which was fuppofed likely to be of ufe in corrupting the heart or mifleading the underftanding. In many of thefe tranflations, certain bolder paffages, which, though well received in Germany, would have excited

cited difguft in England, are wholly omit-
ted, in order that the mind may be more
certainly, though more flowly, prepared
for the full effect of the fame poifon to be
adminiftered in a ftronger degree at another period.

Let not thofe to whom thefe pages
are addreffed deceive themfelves by fuppofing this to be a fable; and let them
inquire moft ferioufly whether I fpeak
truth, in afferting that the attacks of
infidelity in Great Britain are at this
moment principally directed againft the
female breaft. Confcious of the influence
of women in civil fociety, confcious of the
effect which female infidelity produced in
France, they attribute the ill fuccefs of
their attempts in this country, to their
having been hitherto chiefly addreffed to
the male fex. They are now feduloufly
labouring to deftroy the religious principles of women, and in too many inftances
have fatally fucceeded. For this purpofe, not only novels and romances have
been

been made the vehicles of vice and in fidelity, but the fame allurement has been held out to the women of our country, which was employed by the firft philofophift to the firft finner—Knowledge. Liften to the precepts of the new German enlighteners, and you need no longer remain in that fituation in which Providence has placed you! Follow their examples, and you fhall be permitted to indulge in all thofe gratifications which cuftom, not religion, has tolerated in the male fex!

Let us jealoufly watch every deepening fhade in the change of manners; let us mark every ftep, however inconfiderable, whofe tendency is downwards. Corruption is neither ftationary nor retrograde; and to have departed from modefty, is already to have made a progrefs. It is not only awfully true, that fince the new principles have been afloat, *women* have been too eagerly inquifitive after thefe monftrous compofitions; but it is true alfo that, with a new and offenfive renunciation
of

KNOWLEDGE
AS AN
ESCAPE a
from fated
Situation.

of their native delicacy, *many women of cha-*
racter make little hefitation in avowing their
familiarity with works abounding with principles, fentiments, and defcriptions, "which
" fhould not be fo much as named among
" them." By allowing their minds to come
in contact with fuch contagious matter,
they are irrecoverably tainting them ; and
by acknowledging that they are actually
converfant with fuch corruptions, (with
whatever reprobation of the author they
may qualify their perufal of the book,) they
are exciting in others a·moft mifchievous
curiofity for the fame unhallowed gratification. Thus they are daily diminifhing in
the young and the timid thofe wholefome
fcruples, by which, when a tender confcience ceafes to be intrenched, all the
fubfequent ftages of ruin are gradually
facilitated.

We have hitherto fpoken only of the
German *writings ;* but becaufe there are
multitudes who feldom read, equal pains
have been taken to promote the fame object
through

through the medium of the ſtage : and this
weapon is, of all others, that againſt which
it is, at the preſent moment, the moſt im‑
portant to warn the more inconſiderate of
my countrywomen.

As a ſpecimen of the German drama, it
may not be unſeaſonable to offer a few
remarks on the admired play of the
Stranger. In this piece the character of
an *adultreſs*, which, in all periods of the
world, ancient as well as modern, in all
countries, heathen as well as chriſtian, has
hitherto been held in deteſtation, and has
never been introduced but to be repro‑
bated, is for the firſt time preſented to
our view in the moſt pleaſing and faſcinat‑
ing colours. The heroine is a woman
who forſook a huſband the moſt affection‑
ate and the moſt amiable, and lived for
ſome time in the moſt criminal commerce
with her ſeducer. Repenting at length of
her crime, ſhe buries herſelf in retirement.
The talents of the poet during the whole
piece are exerted in attempting to render
this

this woman the object not only of the compaſſion and forgivenefs, but of the efteem and affection of the audience. The injured huſband, convinced of his wife's repentance, forms a refolution, which every man of true feeling and chriſtian piety will probably approve. He forgives her offence, and promiſes her through life his advice, protection, and fortune, together with every thing which can alleviate the miſery of her fituation, but refuſes to replace her in the fituation of his wife. But this is not fufficient for the *German* author. His efforts are employed, and it is to be feared but too fuccefsfully, in making the audience confider the huſband as an unrelenting favage, while they are led by the art of the poet anxiouſly to wiſh to fee an adultrefs reftored to that rank of women who have not violated the moft folemn covenant that can be made with man, nor difobeyed one of the moft pofitive laws which has been enjoined by God.

About

About the fame time that this firft attempt at reprefenting an adultrefs in an exemplary light was made by a German dramatift, which forms an æra in manners ; a direct vindication of adultery was for the firft time attempted by a *woman*, a profeffed admirer and imitator of the German fuicide Werter. *The Female Werter*, as fhe is ftyled by her biographer, afferts, in a work intitled " The Wrongs " of Women," that adultery is juftifiable, and that the reftrictions placed on it by the laws of England conftitute one of the *Wrongs of Women*.

And this leads me to dwell a little longer on this moft deftructive clafs in the whole wide range of modern corruptors, who effect the moft defperate work of the paffions, without fo much as pretending to urge their violence in extenuation of the guilt of indulging them. They folicit this very indulgence with a fort of cold-blooded fpeculation, and invite the

reader

reader to the moſt unbounded gratifications, with all the ſaturnine coolneſs of a
geometrical calculation. Theirs is an ini-
quity rather of phlegm than of ſpirit : and
in the peſtilent atmoſphere they raiſe about
them, as in the infernal climate deſcribed
by Milton,

> The parching air *
> Burns frore, and froſt performs th' effect of fire.

This cool, calculating, intellectual wickedneſs eats out the very heart and core of
virtue, and like a deadly mildew blights
and ſhrivels the blooming promiſe of the
human ſpring. Its benumbing touch com-
municates a torpid ſluggiſhneſs which pa-
ralyzes the ſoul. It deſcants on depravity
as gravely, and details its groſſeſt acts as
frigidly, as if its object were to *allay* the tumult of the paſſions, while it is letting them
looſe on mankind, by " plucking off the
" muzzle" of preſent reſtraint and future

---

* " When the north-wind bloweth it devoureth the
" mountains, and burneth the wilderneſs, and conſum-
" eth the graſs as fire." Eccluſ. xl. 20.

account-

accountablenefs. The fyftem is a dire infufion compounded of bold impiety, bru-
tifh fenfuality, and exquifite folly, which
creeping fatally about the heart, checks the
moral circulation, and totally ftops the
pulfe of goodnefs by the extinction of the
vital principle. Thus not only choaking
the ftream of actual virtue, but drying up
the very fountain of future remorfe and
remote repentance.

The ravages which fome of the old of-
fenders againft purity made in the youthful heart, by the exercife of a fervid but
licentious imagination on the paffions,
was like the mifchief effected by floods,
cataracts, and volcanos. The defolation
indeed was terrible, and the ruin was tremendous: yet it was a ruin which did
not *infallibly* preclude the poffibility of re-
covery. The country, though deluged and
devaftated, was not utterly put beyond the
power of reftoration. The harvefts indeed
were deftroyed, and all was wide fterility.
But, though the crops were loft, the *feeds*

of

of vegetation were not abfolutely eradicated; fo that, after a long and barren
blank, fertility *might* finally return.

But the heart once infected with this
newly medicated venom, fubtil though
fluggifh in its operation, refembles what
travellers relate of that blafted fpot the
dead fea, where thofe devoted cities once
flood which for their pollutions were burnt
with fire from heaven. It continues a
ftagnant lake of putrifying waters. No
wholefome blade ever more fhoots up; the
air is fo tainted that no living thing fubfifts
within its influence. Near the fulphureous
pool the very principle of life is anni-
hilated.—All is death,

<blockquote>Death, unrepealable, eternal death!</blockquote>

But let us take comfort. Thefe projects
are not yet generally realifed. Thefe
atrocious principles are not yet adopted
into common practice. Though corruptions
feem with a confluent tide to be pouring
in upon us from every quarter, yet there
is ftill left among us a difcriminating judgment.

ment. Clear and ſtrongly marked dif-
tinctions between right and wrong ſtill
ſubſiſt. While we continue to cheriſh
this ſanity of mind, the caſe is not deſpe-
rate. Though that crime, the growth of
which always exhibits the moſt irrefragable
proof of the diſſoluteneſs of public manners ; though that crime, which cuts up
order and virtue by the roots, and vioiates
the ſanctity of vows, is awfully increaſing,

> 'Till ſenates ſeem,
> For purpoſes of empire leſs conven'd
> Than to releaſe the adult'reſs from her bonds;

(ſurving)

yet, thanks to the ſurviving efficacy of
a holy religion, to the operation of virtuous laws, and to the energy and unſhaken
integrity with which theſe laws are *now*
adminiſtered ; and, moſt of all perhaps, to
a ſtandard of morals which continues
in force, when the principles which
fanctioned it are no more ; this crime,
in the female ſex at leaſt, is ſtill held
in juſt abhorrence ; if it be practiſed, it is
not honourable ; if it be committed, it
is

is not juftified; we do not yet affect to palliate its turpitude; as yet it hides its abhorred head in lurking privacy; and reprobation *hitherto* follows its publicity.

But on your exerting your influence, with juft application and increafing energy, may in no fmall degree depend whether this corruption fhall ftill continue to be refifted. For, from admiring to adopting, the ftep is fhort, and the progrefs rapid; and it is in the moral as in the natural world; the motion, in the cafe of minds as well as of bodies, is accelerated as they approach the centre to which they are tending.

O ye to whom this addrefs is particularly directed! an awful charge is, in this inftance, committed to your hands; as you difcharge it or fhrink from it, you promote or injure the honour of your daughters and the happinefs of your fons, of both which you are the depofitaries. And, while you refolutely perfevere in making a ftand againft the

E 3 encroach-

encroachments of this crime, fuffer not
your firmnefs to be fhaken by that affectation of charity, which is growing into
a general fubftitute for principle. Abufe
not fo noble a quality as Chriftian candour, by mifemploying it in inftances
to which it does not apply. Pity the
wretched woman you dare not countenance ; and blefs HIM who has " made
" you to differ." If unhappily fhe be
your relation or friend, anxioufly watch
for the period when fhe fhall be deferted
by her betrayer ; and fee if, by your
Chriftian offices, fhe can be fnatched from
a perpetuity of vice.   But if, through the
Divine blefling on your patient endeavours,
fhe fhould ever be awakened to remorfe,
be not anxious to reftore the forlorn
penitent to that fociety againft whofe laws
fhe has fo grievoufly offended ; and remember, that her foliciting fuch a reftoration, furnifhes but too plain a proof that
fhe is not the penitent your partiality would
believe ; fince penitence is more anxious

tc

to make its peace with Heaven than with the world. Joyfully would a truly contrite fpirit commute an earthly for an everlafting reprobation! To reftore a criminal to public fociety, is perhaps to tempt her to repeat her crime, or to deaden her repentance for having committed it. as well as to injure that fociety.; while to reftore a ftrayed foul to God will add luftre to your Chriftian character, and brighten your eternal crown.

In the mean time. there are other evils, ultimately perhaps tending to this, into which we are falling, through that fort of fafhionable candour which, as was hinted above, is among the mifchievous characteriftics of the prefent day ; of which period perhaps it is not the fmalleft evil, that vices are made to look fo like virtues, and are fo affimilated to them, that it requires watchfulnefs and judgment fufficiently to analyze and difcriminate. There are certain women of good fafhion who practife irregularities not confiftent with the ftrictnefs of virtue ;

while

while their good fenfe and knowledge of
the world make them at the fame time
keenly alive to the value of reputation.
They want to retain their indulgences,
without quite forfeiting their credit; but
finding their fame faft declining, they art-
fully cling, by flattery and marked attentions, to a few perfons of more than ordinary character; and thus, till they are
driven to let go their hold, continue to
prop a falling fame.

On the other hand, there are not wanting women of diftinction, of very correct
general conduct, and of no ordinary fenfe
and virtue, who, confiding with a high
mind on what they too confidently call
the integrity of their own hearts; anxious
to deferve a good fame on the one
hand, by a life free from reproach, yet
fecretly too defirous on the other of
fecuring a worldly and fafhionable reputation; while their general affociates
are perfons of honour, and their general refort places of fafety; yet allow themfelves

felves to be occafionally prefent at the
midnight orgies of revelry and gaming,
in houfes of no honourable eftimation;
and thus help to keep up characters,
which, without their fuftaining hand,
would fink to their juft level of contempt
and reprobation. While they are hold-
ing out this plank to a drowning reputation, rather, it is to be feared, fhewing
their own ftrength than affifting another's weaknefs, they value themfelves,
perhaps, on not partaking of the worft
parts of the amufements which may be
carrying on; but they fanction them by
their prefence; they lend their countenance to corruptions they fhould abhor,
and their example to the young and inex-
perienced, who are looking about for
fome fuch fanction to juftify them in
that to which they were before inclined,
but were too timid to have ventured upon
without the protection of fuch unfullied
names. Thus thefe refpectable characters,
without looking to the general confequences

quences of their indifcretion, are thought-
lefsly employed in breaking down, as it
were, the broad fence which fhould ever
feparate two very different forts of fociety,
and are becoming a kind of unnatural link
between vice and virtue.

There is a grofs deception which even
perfons of reputation practife on them
felves. They loudly condemn vice and
irregularity as an abftract principle, nay
they ftigmatize them in perfons of an oppofite party, or in thofe from whom they
themfelves have no profpect of perfonal
advantage or amufement, and in whom
therefore they have no particular intereft
to tolerate evil. But the fame diforders
are viewed without abhorrence when prac-
tifed by thofe who in any way minifter to
their pleafures. Refined entertainments,
luxurious decorations, felect mufic, whatever furnifhes any delight rare and exquifite to the fenfes, thefe foften the feverity
of criticifm; thefe palliate fins, varnifh
over the flaws of a broken character, and
extort

extort not pardon merely, but juftifi-
cation, countenance, intimacy! The more
refpectable will not, perhaps, go all the
length of vindicating the difreputable vice,
but they affect to difbelieve its exiftence
in the individual inftance; or, failing in
this, they will bury its acknowledged turpitude in the feducing qualities of the
agreeable delinquent. Talents of every
kind are confidered as a commutation for
a few vices, and fuch are made a paffport
to introduce into honourable fociety characters whom their profligacy ought to exclude from it.

But the great object to which you who
are, or may be mothers, are more efpecially called, is the education of your
children. If we are refponfible for the
ufe of influence in the cafe of thofe over
whom we have no immediate control, in
the cafe of our children we are refponfible
for the exercife of acknowledged power;
a power wide in its extent, indefinite in its
effects, and ineftimable in its importance.

On

On you, depend in no fmall degree the
principles of the whole rifing generation.
To your direction the daughters are
almoft exclufively committed; and until a
certain age, to you alfo is configned the
mighty privilege of forming the hearts
and minds of your infant fons. By the
bleffing of God on the principles you
fhall, as far as it depends on you, infufe
into both fons and daughters, they will
hereafter " arife and call you bleffed."
And in the great day of general account,
may every Chriftian mother be enabled
through divine grace to fay, with humble
confidence, to her Maker and Redeemer,
" Behold the children whom thou haft
" given me!"

Chriftianity, driven out from the reft
of the world, has ftill, bleffed be God!
a " ftrong hold" in this country. And
though it be the fpecial duty of the appointed " watchman, *now* that he feeth
" the fword come upon the land, to
" blow the trumpet and warn the people,
" which

" which if he neglect to do, their blood
" fhall be required of the watchman's
" hand * :" yet, in this facred garrifon,
impregnable but by neglect, YOU too have
an awful poft, that of arming the
minds of the rifing generation with the
" fhield of faith, whereby they fhall be
" able to quench the fiery darts of the
" wicked ;" that of girding them with
" that fword of the Spirit which is the
" word of God." If you neglect this
your bounden duty, you will have effectually contributed to expel Chriftianity
from her laft citadel. And, remember,
that the dignity of the work to which you
are called, is no lefs than that of preferv-
ing the ark of the Lord.

* Ezekiel, xxxiii. 6.

CHAP. II.

On the education of women.—The prevailing system tends to establish the errors which it ought to correct.—Dangers arising from an excessive cultivation of the arts.

IT is far from being the object of this flight work to offer a regular plan of female education, a task which has been often more properly assumed by far abler writers; but it is intended rather to suggest a few remarks on the reigning mode, which, though it has had many panegyrists, appears to be defective, not only in a few particulars, but as a general system. There are indeed numberless honourable exceptions to an observation which will be thought severe; yet the author questions if it be not the natural and direct tendency of the prevailing and popular system, to excite and promote those very defects

4   which

which it ought to be the main end and object of Chriftian education to remove; whether, inftead of directing this important engine to attack and deftroy *vanity, felfifh-nefs, and inconfideration*, that triple alliance in ftrict and conftant league againft female virtue; the combined powers of inftruction are not feduloufly confederated in confirming their ftrength and eftablifhing their empire?

If indeed the *material* fubftance, if the body and limbs, with the organs and fenfes, be really the more valuable objects of attention, then there is little room for animadverfion and improvement. But if the immaterial and immortal mind; if the heart, " out of which are the iffues of " life," be the main concern; if the great bufinefs of education be to implant ideas, to communicate knowledge, to form a correct tafte and a found judgment, to refift evil propenfities, and, above all, to feize the favourable feafon for infufing principles and confirming habits; if education be

be a school to fit us for life, and life be a
school to fit us for eternity; if such, I repeat it, be the chief work and grand ends of
education, it may then be worth inquiring
how far these ends are likely to be effected
by the prevailing system.

Is it not a fundamental error to consider
children as innocent beings, whose little
weaknesses may perhaps want some cor-
rection, rather than as beings who bring
into the world a corrupt nature and evil
dispositions, which it should be the great
end of education to rectify? This appears
to be such a foundation-truth, that if
I were asked what quality is most important in an instructor of youth, I should
not hesitate to reply, *such a strong im-*
pression of the corruption of our nature, as
should insure a disposition to counteract it ;
together with such a deep view and thorough
knowledge of the human heart, as should
be necessary for developing and controlling its
most secret and complicated workings. And
let us remember that to *know the world,*

15   as

as it is called, that is, to know its local manners, temporary ufages, and evanefcent fafhions, is not to *know human nature*: and that where this prime knowledge is wanting, thofe natural evils which ought to be counteracted will be foftered.

Vanity, for inftance, is reckoned among the light and venial errors of youth ; nay, fo far from being treated as a dangerous enemy, it is often called in as an auxiliary. At worft, it is confidered as a harmlefs weaknefs, which fubtracts little from the value of a character; as a natural effervefcence, which will fubfide of itfelf, when the firft ferment of the youthful paffions fhall have done working. But thofe know little of the conformation of the human and efpecially of the female heart, who fancy that vanity is ever exhaufted, by the mere operation of time and events. Let thofe who maintain this opinion look into our places of public refort, and there behold if the ghoft of departed beauty is not to its laft flitting fond of haunting the

fcenes

ſcenes of its paſt pleaſures; the ſoul, unwilling (if I may borrow an alluſion from
the Platonic mythology) to quit the ſpot
in which the body enjoyed its former
delights, ſtill continues to hover about the
ſame place, though the ſame pleaſures are
no longer to be found there. Diſappoint-
ments indeed may divert vanity into a
new direction; prudence may prevent it
from breaking out into exceſſes, and age
may prove that it is " vexation of ſpirit;"
but neither diſappointment, prudence, nor
age can *cure* it; for they do not correct
the principle. Nay, the very diſappointment itſelf ſerves as a painful evidence of
its protracted exiſtence.

Since then there is a ſeaſon when the
youthful muſt ceaſe to be young, and the
beautiful to excite admiration; to learn how
to grow old gracefully is perhaps one of the
rareſt and moſt valuable arts which can be
taught to woman. It is for this ſober ſeaſon of life that education ſhould lay up its
rich reſources. However diſregarded they
may

may hitherto have been, they will be
wanted now. When admirers fall away,
and flatterers become mute, the mind will
be driven to retire into itself, and if it find
no entertainment at home, it will be driven
back again upon the world with increafed
force. Yet forgetting this, do we not
feem to educate our daughters, exclufively,
for the tranfient period of youth, when it
is to maturer life we ought to advert?
Do we not educate them for a crowd,
forgetting that they are to live at home?
for the world, and not for themfelves? for
fhow, and not for ufe? for time, and not
for eternity?

Vanity (and the fame may be faid of
felfifhnefs) is not to be refifted like any
other vice, which is fometimes bufy and
fometimes quiet; it is not to be attacked
as a fingle fault, which is indulged in
oppofition to a fingle virtue; but it is
uniformly to be controlled, as an active, a
reftlefs, a growing principle, at conftant
war with all the Chriftian graces; which

F 2   not

not only mixes itfelf with all our faults, but infinuates itfelf into all our virtues too ; and will, if not checked effectually, rob our beſt actions of their reward. Vanity, if I may ufe the analogy, is, with refpect to the other vices, what feeling is in regard to the other fenfes ; it is not confined in its operation to the eye, or the ear, or any fingle organ, but diffufed through the whole being, alive in every part, awakened and communicated by the flighteſt touch.

Not a few of the evils of the prefent day arife from a new and perverted application of terms ; among thefe, perhaps, there is not one more abufed, mifunderſtood, or mifapplied, than the term *accomplishments.* This word in its original meaning fignifies *completenefs, perfection.* But I may fafely appeal to the obfervation of mankind, whether they do not meet with fwarms of youthful females, iſſuing from our board-ing fchools, as well as emerging from the more private fcenes of domeſtic education,

who

who are introduced into the world, under the broad and univerſal title of *accompliſhed young ladies*, of *all* of whom it cannot very truly and correctly be pronounced, that they illuſtrate the definition by a complete-neſs which leaves nothing to be added, and a perfection which leaves nothing to be deſired. ——→ *they are "complete" before marriage?*

This phrenzy of accompliſhments, un-happily, is no longer restricted within the uſual limits of rank and fortune ; the middle orders have caught the contagion, and it rages downward with increaſing and destructive violence, from the elegantly dreſſed but ſlenderly portioned curate's daughter, to the equally faſhionable daugh-ter of the little tradeſman, and of the more opulent but not more judicious farmer. And is it not obvious, that as far as this epidemical mania has ſpread, this very va-luable part of ſociety is declining in uſe-fulneſs, as it riſes in its unlucky pretenſions to elegance ? till this rapid revolution of the manners of the middle claſs has ſo far

altered

altered the character of the age, as to be in
danger of rendering obfolete the heretofore
common faying, " that moft worth and
" virtue are to be found in the middle fta-
" tion." For I do not fcruple to affert,
that in general, as far as my little obfervation has extended, this clafs of females,
in what relates both to religious knowledge
and to practical induftry, falls fhort both
of the very high and the very low. Their
new courfe of education, and the habits of
life and elegance of drefs connected with it,
peculiarly unfits them for the active duties
of their own very important condition ;
while, with frivolous eagernefs, and fecond-
hand opportunities, they run to fnatch
a few of thofe fhowy acquirements which
decorate the great. This is done apparently with one or other of thefe views ;
either to make their fortune by marriage,
or if that fail, to qualify them to become
teachers of others : hence the abundant
multiplication of fuperficial wives, and
of incompetent and illiterate governeffes,

I   The

The ufe of the pencil, the performance of exquifite but unneceffary works, the ftudy of foreign languages and of mufic, require (with fome exceptions which fhould always be made in favour of great natural genius) a degree of leifure which belongs exclufively to affluence *. One ufe of learning languages is, not that we may know what the terms which exprefs the articles of our drefs and our table are called in French or Italian; not that we may think over a few ordinary phrafes in Eng-lifh, and then tranflate them, without one foreign idiom; for he who cannot *think* in a language cannot be faid to underftand it: but the great ufe of acquiring any foreign language is, either that it enables us oc-cafionally to converfe with foreigners, unac-quainted with any other, or that it is a key to the literature of the country to which it

---

* Thofe among the clafs in queftion, whofe own good fenfe leads them to avoid thefe miftaken pur-fuits, cannot be offended at a reproof which does not belong to them.

F 4 belongs;

belongs; and thofe humbler females, the chief part of whofe time is required for do-meftic offices, are little likely to fall in the way of foreigners; and fo far from enjoying opportunities for the acquifition of foreign literature, they have feldom time to poffefs themfelves of all that valuable knowledge which the books of their own country fo abundantly furnifh; and the acquifition of which would be fo much more ufeful and honourable than the paltry acceffions they make, by hammering out the meaning of a few paffages in a tongue they but imper-fectly underftand, and of which they are likely to make no ufe.

It would be well if the reflection how eagerly this redundancy of accomplifh-ments is feized on by their inferiors, were to operate as in the cafe of other abfurd fafhions; the rich and great being feldom brought to renounce any mode or cuftom, from the mere confideration that it is pre-pofterous, or that it is wrong; while they are frightened into its immediate relinquifh-

ment,

ment, from the preffing confideration that
the *vulgar* are beginning to adopt it.

But, to return to that more elevated,
and, on account of their more extended
influence only, that more important clafs
of females, to whofe ufe this little work
is more immediately dedicated. Some
popular authors, on the fubject of female
inftruction, had for a time eftablifhed a
fantaftic code of artificial manners. They
had refined elegance into infipidity,
frittered down delicacy into frivoloufnefs,
and reduced manner into *minauderie*. But
" to lifp, and to amble, and to nick-name
" God's creatures," has nothing to do
with true gentlenefs of mind ; and to be
filly makes no neceffary part of foftnefs.
Another clafs of cotemporary authors
turned all the force of their talents to excite *emotions*, to infpire *fentiment*, and to reduce all mental and moral excellence into
fympathy and *feeling*. Thefe fofter qualities
were elevated at the expence of principle ;
and young women were inceffantly hearing
unqualified

unqualified fenfibility extolled as the perfection of their nature; till thofe who
really poffeffed this amiable quality, inftead
of directing, and chaftifing, and reftrain-
ing it, were in danger of foftering it to
their hurt, and began to confider themfelves as deriving their excellence from its
excefs; while thofe lefs interefting damfels,
who happened not to find any of this amiable fenfibility in their *hearts*, but thought
it creditable to have it fomewhere, fancied
its feat was in the *nerves;* and here
indeed it was eafily found or feigned;
till a falfe and exceffive difplay of feeling
became fo predominant, as to bring in
queftion the actual exiftence of that true
tendernefs, without which, though a
woman may be worthy, fhe can never be
amiable.

Fafhion then, by one of her fudden
and rapid turns, inftantaneoufly ftruck out
both real fenfibility and the affectation of it
from the ftanding lift of female perfections;
and, by a quick touch of her magic wand,
fhifted

fhifted the fcene, and at once produced
the bold and independent beauty, the
intrepid female, the hoyden, the huntrefs,
and the archer; the fwinging arms, the
confident addrefs, the regimental, and
the four-in-hand. Such felf-complacent
heroines made us ready to regret their
fofter predeceffors, who had aimed only at
pleafing the other fex, while thefe afpiring
fair ones ftruggled for the bolder renown
of rivalling them; the project failed;
for, whereas the former had fued for admiration, the latter challenged, feized,
compelled it; but the men, as was natural, continued to prefer the more modeft
claimant to the fturdy competitor.

It were well if we, who have the advantage of contemplating the errors of the
two extremes, were to look for truth where
fhe is commonly to be found, in the plain
and obvious middle path, equally remote
from each excefs; and, while we bear in
mind that helpleffnefs is not delicacy, let
us alfo remember that mafculine manners
do not neceffarily include ftrength of
character

character nor vigour of intellect. Should
we not reflect alfo, that we are neither
to train up Amazons nor Circaffians, but
that it is our bufinefs to form Chriftians?
that we have to educate not only rational,
but accountable beings? and, remembering this, fhould we not be folicitous to let
our daughters learn of the well-taught, and
affociate with the well-bred? In training
them, fhould we not carefully cultivate intellect, implant religion, and cherifh modefty? Then, whatever is engaging in
manners would be the natural refult of
whatever is juft in fentiment, and correct
in principle; foftnefs would grow out of
humility, and external delicacy would
fpring from purity of heart : then the de-
corums, the proprieties, the elegancies, and
even the graces, as far as they are fimple,
pure, and honeft, would follow as an almoft
inevitable confequence; for to follow in
the train of the Chriftian virtues, and not
to take the lead of them, is the proper
place which religion affigns to the
graces.

Whether

Whether we have made the beſt uſe of the errors of our predeceſſors, and of our own numberleſs advantages, and whether the prevailing ſyſtem be really conſiſtent with ſound policy, true taſte, or Chriſtian principle, it may be worth our while to inquire.

Would not a ſtranger be led to imagine by a view of the reigning mode of female education, that human life conſiſted of one univerſal holiday, and that the grand con-teſt between the ſeveral competitors was, who ſhould be moſt eminently qualified to excel, and carry off the prize, in the various ſhows and games which were intended to be exhibited in it ? And to the exhibitors themſelves, would he not be ready to apply Sir Francis Bacon's obſervation on the Olympian victors, that they were ſo excellent in theſe unneceſſary things, that their perfection muſt needs have been acquired by the neglect of whatever was neceſſary ?

What

What would the polifhed Addifon, who thought that one great end of a lady's learning to dance was, that fhe might know how to fit ftill gracefully ; what would even the Pagan hiftorian * of the great Roman confpirator, who could commemorate it among the defects of his hero's *accomplifhed* miftrefs, " that fhe was " too good a finger and dancer for a " virtuous woman ;"—what would thefe refined critics have faid, had they lived as we have done, to fee the art of dancing lifted into fuch importance, that it cannot with any degree of fafety be confided to one inftructor, but a whole train of fucceffive mafters are confidered as abfo- lutely effential to its perfection ? What would thefe accurate judges of female manners have faid, to fee a modeft young lady firft delivered into the hands of a military ferjeant to inftruct her in the *feminine* art of marching ? and when this

* Salluft.

delicate

delicate acquisition is attained, to see her
transferred to a profeffor, who is to teach
her the Scotch fteps; which profeffor,
having communicated his indifpenfable
portion of this indifpenfable art, makes
way for the profeffor of French dances;
and all perhaps, in their turn, either yield
to, or have the honour to co-operate with,
a finifhing mafter; each probably receiv-
ing a ftipend which would make the pious
curate or the learned chaplain rich and
happy?

The fcience of mufic, which ufed to
be communicated in fo competent a degree to a young lady by one able inftructor,
is now diftributed among a whole band.
She now requires, not a mafter, but an
orcheftra. And my country readers would
accufe me of exaggeraion were I to hazard
enumerating the variety of mufical teachers
who attend at the fame time in the fame family; the daughters of which are fum-
moned, by at leaft as many inftruments as
the fubjects of Nebuchadnezzar, to worfhip
the

the idol which fafhion has fet up. They would be incredulous were I to produce real inftances. in which the delighted mother has been heard to declare, that the vifits of mafters of every art and the different mafters for various gradations of the fame art, followed each other in fuch clofe and rapid fucceffion during the whole London refidence, that her girls had not a moment's interval to look into a book ; nor could fhe contrive any method to introduce one, till fhe happily devifed the fcheme of reading to them herfelf for half an hour while they were drawing, by which means no time was loft *.

Before

* Since the firft edition of this Work appeared, the author has received from a perfon of great eminence the following ftatement, afcertaining the *time* employed in the aequifition of mufic in one inftance. As a *general* calculation, it will perhaps be found to be fo far from exaggerated, as to be below the truth. The ftatement concludes with remarking, that the individual who is the fubject of it is now married to a man who *diflikes mufic!*

Suppofe

Before the evil is paſt redreſs, it will be prudent to reflect that in all poliſhed countries an entire devotedneſs to the fine arts has been one grand ſource of the corruption of the women; and ſo juſtly were theſe pernicious conſequences appreciated by the Greeks, among whom theſe arts were carried to the higheſt poſſible perfection, that they ſeldom allowed them to be cultivated to a very exquiſite degree by women of great purity of character. And if the ambition of an elegant Britiſh lady ſhould be fired by the idea that the accompliſhed females of thoſe poliſhed ſtates were the admired companions of the philoſophers, the poets, the wits, and the

---

Suppoſe your pupil to begin at ſix years of age, and to continue at the average of four hours a-day *only*, Sunday excepted, and thirteen days allowed for travelling annually, till ſhe is eighteen, the ſtate ſtands thus: 300 days multiplied by four, the number of hours amount to 1200; that number multiplied by twelve, which is the number of years, amounts to 14,400 hours!

　　　artiſts

artifts of Athens; and their beauty or talents, fo much the favourite fubjects of the mufe, the lyre, the pencil, and the chiffel; that their pictures and ftatues furnifhed the moft confummate models of Grecian art: if, I fay, the accomplifhed females of our days are panting for fimilar renown, let their modefty chaftife their ambition, by recollecting that thefe cele-brated women are not to be found among the chafte women and the virtuous daugh-ters of the Ariftides's, the Agis's, and the Phocions; but that they are to be looked for among the Phrynes, the Lais's, the Afpafias, and the Glyceras. I am per-fuaded the Chriftian female, whatever be her tafte or her talents, will renounce the defire of any celebrity when attached to impurity of character, with the fame noble indignation with which the virtuous bio-grapher of the above-named heroes re-nounced any kind of difhoneft fame, by exclaiming, " I had rather it fhould be faid " there never was a Plutarch, than that " they

" they fhould fay Plutarch was malignant,
" unjuft, or envious *."

And while this corruption, brought on
by an exceffive cultivation of the arts,
has contributed its full fhare to the decline
of ftates, it has always furnifhed an infallible fymptom of their impending fall.
The fatires of the moft penetrating and
judicious of the Roman poets, corroborat-
ing the teftimonies of the moft accurate
of their hiftorians, abound with invectives
againft the general depravity of manners
introduced by the corrupt habits of female
education. The bitternefs and grofs
indelicacy of fome of thefe fatirifts (too
grofs to be either quoted or referred to)
make little againft their authority in thefe
points ; for how fhocking muft thofe corruptions have been, and how obvioufly
offenfive their caufes, which could have

* No cenfure is levelled at the exertions of real
genius, which is as valuable as it is rare; but at the
abfurdity of that fyftem which is erecting *the who't
fex* into artifts.

appeared

appeared fo highly difgufting to minds fo coarfe as not likely to be fcandalized by flight deviations from decency! The famous ode of Horace, attributing the vices and difafters of his degenerate country to the fame caufe, might, were it quite free from the above objections, be produced, I will not prefume to fay as an exact picture of the exifting manners of this country; but may I not venture to fay, as a prophecy, the fufilment of which cannot be very remote? It may however be obferved, that the modefty of the Roman matron, and the chafte demeanor of her virgin daughters, which amidft the ftern virtues of the ftate were as immaculate and pure as the honour of the Roman citizen, fell a facrifice to the luxurious diffipation brought in by their Afiatic conquefts; after which the females were foon taught a complete change of character. They were inftructed to accommodate their talents of pleafing to the more vitiated taftes of the other fex; and began to

ftudy

ftudy every grace and every art which
might captivate the exhaufted hearts,
and excite the wearied and capricious in-
clinations of the men; till by a rapid and
at length complete enervation, the Roman
charaĉter loft its fignature, and through a
quick fucceffion of flavery, effeminacy, and
vice, funk into that degeneracy of which
fome of the modern Italian ftates ferve to
furnifh a too juft fpecimen.

It is of the effence of human things
that the fame objeĉts which are highly
ufeful in their feafon, meafure, and degree, become mifchievous in their excefs,
at other periods and under other circumftances. In a ftate of barbarifm, the arts
are among the beft reformers; and they
go on to be improved themfelves, and
improving thofe who cultivate them, till,
having reached a certain point, thofe
very arts which were the inftruments
of civilization and refinement, become
inftruments of corruption and decay;
enervating and depraving in the fecond
inftance, by the excefs and univerfality of

7 EXCESS.

their

their cultivation, as certainly as they refined in the firſt. They become agents of voluptuouſneſs. They excite the imagination; and the imagination thus excited, and no longer under the government of ſtrict principle, becomes the moſt dangerous ſtimulant of the paſſions; promotes a too keen reliſh for pleaſure, teaching how to multiply its ſources, and inventing new and pernicious modes of artificial gratification.

May we not rank among the preſent corrupt conſequences of this unbounded cultivation, the unchaſte *coſtume*, the impure ſtyle of dreſs, and that indelicate ſtatue-like exhibition of the female figure, which by its artfully-diſpoſed folds, its ſeemingly wet and adheſive drapery, ſo defines the form as to prevent covering itſelf from becoming a veil? This licentious mode, as the acute Monteſquieu obſerved on the dances of the Spartan virgins, has taught us " to ſtrip chaſtity itſelf of " modeſty."

May

May the author be allowed to addrefs
to our own country and our own circumftances, to both of which they feem
peculiarly applicable, the fpirit of that
beautiful apoftrophe of the moft polifhed
poet of antiquity to the moft victorious
nation ? " Let us leave to the inhabitants
" of *conquered countries* the praife of
" carrying to the very higheft degree
" of perfection, fculpture and the fifter
" arts; but let *this* country direct her
" own exertions to the art of govern-
" ing mankind in equity and peace,
" of fhewing mercy to the fubmiffive,
" and of abafing the proud among fur-
" rounding nations *."

* Let me not be fufpected of bringing into any
fort of comparifon the gentlenefs of Britifh government with the rapacity of Roman conquefts, or the
principles of Roman dominion. To fpoil, to butcher,
and to commit every kind of violence, they call, fays
one of the ableft of their hiftorians, by the lying name
of *government*, and when they have fpread a general
defolation, they call it *peace* (1).

(1) Tacitus' Life of Agricola, fpeech of Galgacus to his
foldiers.

With

With fuch *dictatorial*, or, as we might now read, *directorial* inquifitors, *we* can have no point of contact; and if I have applied the fervile flattery of a delightful poet to the purpofe of Englifh happinefs, it was only to fhew wherein true national grandeur confifts, and that every country pays too dear a price for thofe arts and embellifhments of fociety which endanger the lofs of its morals and manners.

CHAP. III.

External Improvement.—Children's Balls.—
French Governesses.

LET me not however be misunderstood.
The customs which fashion has established,
when not in direct opposition to what
is right, should unquestionably be pursued
in the education of ladies. Piety main-
tains no natural war with elegance, and
Christianity would be no gainer by making
her disciples unamiable. Religion does
not forbid that the exterior be made to a
certain degree the object of attention.
But the admiration bestowed, the sums
expended, and the time lavished on
arts which add little to the intrinsic
value of life, should have limitations.
While these arts should be admired, let
them not be admired above their just
value: while they are practised, let it not

be

be to the exclusion of higher employments :
while they are cultivated, let it be to amuse
leisure, not to engross life.

But it happens unfortunately, that to ordinary obfervers, the girl who is really re-
ceiving the worst instruction often makes
the best figure ; while in the more correct but less ostensible education, the deep
and sure foundations to which the edifice
will owe its strength and stability lie out
of sight. The outward accomplishments
have the dangerous advantage of addressing themselves more immediately to the
senses, and of course meet everywhere with
those who can in some measure appreciate
as well as admire them ; for all can see
and hear, but all cannot scrutinize and difcriminate. External acquirements too
recommend themselves the more because
they are more rapidly as well as more vi-
sibly progressive. While the mind is led
on to improvement by slow motions and
imperceptible degrees ; while the heart
must now be admonished by reproof, and
now

now allured by kindnefs ; its livelieft advances being fuddenly impeded by obftinacy, and its brighteft profpects often ob-
fcured by paffion ; it is flow in its acquifitions of virtue, and reluctant in its ap-
proaches to piety. The unruly and tur-
bulent propenfities of the mind are not fo
obedient to the forming hand as defects of
manner or awkwardnefs of gait. Often
when we fancy that a troublefome paffion
is completely crufhed, we have the mortification to find that we have " fcotch'd the
" fnake, not killed it." One evil temper
ftarts up before another is conquered. The
fubduing hand cannot cut off the ever-
fprouting heads fo faft as the prolific Hy-
dra can re-produce them, nor fell the ftub-
born Antæus fo often as he can recruit his
ftrength, and rife in vigorous and repeated
oppofition.

Hired teachers are alfo under a difadvantage refembling tenants at rack-rent ;
it is their intereft to bring in an immediate
revenue of praife and profit, and, for the

4   fake

fake of a prefent rich crop, thofe who are not ftrictly confcientious, do not care how much the ground is impoverifhed for future produce. But parents, who are the lords of the foil, muft look to permanent value, and to continued fruitfulnefs. The beft effects of a careful education are often very remote; they are to be difcovered in future fcenes, and exhibited in as yet untried connexions. Every event of life will be putting the heart into frefh fitu-ations, and making new demands on its prudence, its firmnefs, its integrity, or its forbearance. Thofe whofe bufinefs it is to form and model it, cannot forefee thofe contingent fituations fpecifically and diftinctly; yet, as far as human wifdom will allow, they muft enable it to prepare for them all by general principles, correct habits, and an unremitted fenfe of depend-ence on the Great Difpofer of events. The young Chriftian militant muft learn and practife all his evolutions, though he does not know on what fervice his leader may command him, by what particular

foe

foe he fhall be moft affailed, nor what mode
of attack the enemy may employ.

But the contrary of all this is the
cafe with external acquifitions. The mafter, it is his intereft, will induftrioufly
inftruct his young pupil to fet all her
improvements in the moft immediate and
confpicuous point of view. To attract admiration is the great principle feduloufly
inculcated into her young heart; and is
confidered as the fundamental maxim;
and, perhaps, if we were required to con-
denfe the reigning fyftem of the brilliant
education of a lady into an aphorifm, it
might be comprifed in this fhort fentence,
To allure and to fhine. This fyftem however is the fruitful germ, from which a
thoufand yet unborn vanities, with all their
multiplied ramifications, will fpring. A
tender mother cannot but feel an honeft
triumph in completing thofe talents in her
daughter which will neceffarily excite admiration; but fhe will alfo fhudder at the
vanity that admiration may excite, and at
the

the new ideas it will awaken; and, ſtart-
ling as it may found, the labours of a wiſe
mother anxious for her daughter's beſt intereſts, will ſeem to be at variance with
thoſe of all her teachers. She will indeed
rejoice at her progreſs, but ſhe will rejoice
with trembling; for ſhe is fully aware
that if all poſſible accompliſhments could
be bought at the price of a ſingle virtue,
of a ſingle principle, the purchaſe would
be infinitely dear, and ſhe would rejeĉt the
dazzling but deſtruĉtive acquiſition. She
knows that the ſuperſtruĉture of the accompliſhments can be alone ſafely ereĉted
on the broad and ſolid baſis of Chriſtian
humility: nay more, that as the materials
of which that ſuperſtruĉture is to be com-
poſed, are in themſelves of ſo unſtable and
tottering a nature, the foundation muſt be
deepened and enlarged with more abundant care, otherwiſe the fabric will be
overloaded with its own ornaments, and
what was intended only to embelliſh the
building, will prove the occaſion of its fall.
                                          " To

" To every thing there is a feafon, and
" a time for every purpofe under heaven,"
faid the wife man ; but he faid it before
the invention of baby-balls ; an invention
which has formed a kind of æra in the annals of polifhed education. This modern
device is a fort of triple confpiracy againft
the innocence, the health, and the happinefs of children ; thus, by factitious amufements, to rob them of a relifh for the
fimple joys, the unbought delights, which
naturally belong to their blooming feafon,
is like blotting out fpring from the year.
To facrifice the true and proper enjoyments of fprightly and happy children,
is to make them pay a dear and difpro-
portionate price for their artificial pleafures.
They ftep at once from the nurfery to the
ball-room ; and, by a change of habits as
new as it is prepofterous, are thinking of
dreffing themfelves, at an age when they
ufed to be dreffing their dolls. Inftead of
bounding with the unreftrained freedom of
little

little wood-nymphs, over hill and dale, their cheeks flufhed with health, and their hearts overflowing with happinefs, thefe *gay* little creatures are fhut up all the morning, demurely practifing the *pas grave*, and tranfacting the ferious bufinefs of acquiring a new ftep for the evening, with more coft of time and pains than it would have taken them to acquire twenty new ideas.

Thus they lofe the amufements which naturally belong to their fmiling period, and naturally anticipate thofe pleafures (fuch as they are,) which would come in, too much of courfe, on their introduction into fafhionable life. The true pleafures of childhood are cheap and natural; for every object teems with delight to eyes and hearts new to the enjoyment of life; nay, the hearts of healthy children abound with a general difpofition to mirth and joy-fulnefs, even without a fpecific object to excite it; like our firft parent, in the world's world's firſt ſpring, when all was new, and freſh, and gay about him,

> they live and move,
> And feel that they are happier than they know.

Only furniſh them with a few ſimple and harmleſs materials, and a little, but not too much, leiſure, and they will manufacture their own pleaſures with more ſkill, and ſuccefs, and ſatisfaction, than they will receive from all that your money can purchaſe. Their bodily recreations ſhould be ſuch as will promote their health, quicken their activity, enliven their ſpirits, whet their ingenuity, and qualify them for their mental work. But, if you begin thus early to create wants, to invent gratifications, to multiply deſires, to waken dormant ſenſibilities, to ſtir up hidden fires, you are ſtudiouſly laying up for your children a ſtore of premature caprice, and irritability, and diſcontent.

While childhood preſerves its native ſimplicity, every little change is intereſting, every gratification is a luxury ; a ride or a

walk, a garland of flowers of her own forming, a plant of her own cultivating, will be
a delightful amufement to a child in her
natural ftate; but it will be dull and tafte-
lefs to a fophifticated little creature, nurfed
in thefe forced, and coftly, and vapid pleafures. Alas! that we fhould throw away
this firft grand opportunity of working
into a practical habit the moral of this important truth, that the chief fource of human difcontent is to be looked for, not in
our real, but in our factitious wants; not
in the demands of nature, but in the artificial cravings of defire!

When one fees the growing zeal to
crowd the midnight ball with thefe pretty
fairies, one would be almoft tempted to
fancy it was a kind of pious emulation
among the mothers to cure their infants of
a fondnefs for vain and foolifh pleafures,
by tiring them out by this pre ature
familiarity with them; and that they were
actuated by fomething of the fame principle which led the Spartans to introduce
their fons to fcenes of riot, that they might

conceive

conceive an early difguſt at vice! or
poſſibly, that they imitated thoſe Scythian
mothers who uſed to plunge their new-
born infants into the flood, thinking none
to be worth ſaving who could not ſtand
this early ſtruggle for their lives: the
greater part, indeed, as it might have been
expeɑed, periſhed; but the parents took
comfort, that if many were loſt, the few
who eſcaped would be the ſtronger for
having been thus expoſed.

To behold lilliputian coquettes, projeɑ-
ing dreſſes, ſtudying colours, aſſorting
ribbands and feathers, their little hearts
beating with hopes about partners and
fears about rivals; and to ſee their freſh
cheeks pale after the midnight ſupper,
their aching heads and unbraced nerves,
diſqualifying the little languid beings for
the next day's taſk; and to hear the grave
apology, " that it is owing to the wine, the
" crowd, the heated room of the laſt
" night's ball;" all this, I ſay, would
really be as ludicrous, if the miſchief of

the

the thing did not take off from the merri-
ment of it, as any of the ridiculous and
prepofterous difproportions in the divert-
ing travels of Captain Lemuel Gulliver.

Under a juft impreffion of the evils
which we are fuftaining from the principles and the practices of *modern* France,
we are apt to lofe fight of thofe deep
and lafting mifchiefs which fo long, fo
regularly, and fo fyftematically, we have
been importing from the fame country,
though in another form and under
another government. In one refpect, indeed, the firft were the more formidable,
becaufe we embraced the ruin without fufpecting it ; while we defeat the malignity
of the latter, by detecting the turpitude
and defending ourfelves againft it. This
is not the place to defcant on that levity of
manners, that contempt of the Sabbath,
that fatal familiarity with loofe principles,
and thofe relaxed notions of conjugal
fidelity, which have often been tranfplanted
into this country by women of fafhion,

as

as a too common effect of a long refidence
in that: but it is peculiarly fuitable to
my fubject to advert to another domeftic
mifchief derived from the fame foreign
extraction: I mean, the rifks that have
been run, and the facrifices which have
been made, in order to furnifh our young
ladies with the means of acquiring the
French language in the greateft poffible
purity. Perfection in this accomplifhment
has been fo long eftablifhed as the fupreme
object; fo long confidered as the predominant excellence to which all other
excellencies muft bow down, that it would
be hopelefs to attack a law which fafhion
has immutably decreed, and which has
received the ftamp of long prefcription.
We muft, therefore, be contented with ex-
preffing a wifh, that this indifpenfable perfection could have been attained at the
expence of facrifices lefs important.   It is
with the greater regret I animadvert on
this and fome other prevailing practices,
as they are errors into which the wife

H 3   and

and refpectable have, through want of confideration, or rather through want of firmnefs to refift the tyranny of fafhion, fometimes fallen. It has not been unufual when mothers of rank and reputation have been afked how they ventured to intruft their daughters to foreigners, of whofe principles they knew nothing, except that they were Roman Catholics, to anfwer, " That they had taken care to be fecure " on that fubject; for that it had been " ftipulated that *the queftion of religion* " *fhould never be agitated between the* " *teacher and the pupil.*" This, it muft be confeffed, is a moft defperate remedy ; it is like ftarving to death, to avoid being poifoned. And one cannot help trembling for the event of that education, from which religion, as far as the governefs is concerned, is thus formally and fyftematically excluded. Surely it would not be exacting too much, to fuggeft at leaft that an attention no lefs fcrupulous fhould be exerted to infure the character of our children's

children's inſtructor, for piety and knowledge, than is thought neceſſary to aſcertain
that ſhe has nothing *patois* in her dialect.

I would rate a correct pronunciation
and an elegant phraſeology at their juſt
price, and I would not rate them low;
but I would not offer up principle as
a victim to ſounds and accents. And the
matter is now made more eaſy; for whatever diſgrace it might once have brought
on an Engliſh lady to have had it ſuſpected
from her accent that ſhe had the misfortune not to be born in a neighbouring
country; ſome recent events may ſerve to
reconcile her to the ſuſpicion of having
been bred in her own: a country, to
which (with all its ſins, which are many!)
the whole world is looking up with envy
and admiration, as the ſeat of true glory
and of comparative happineſs: a country,
in which the exile, driven out by the crimes
of his own, finds a home; a country, to
obtain the protection of which it was claim
enough to be unfortunate; and no im-
H 4   pediment

pediment to have been the fubject of her
direft foe! a country, which in this refpect humbly imitating the Father of compaffion, when it offered mercy to a fup-
pliant enemy, never conditioned for merit,
nor infifted on the virtues of the miferable
as a preliminary to its own bounty!

CHAP. IV

Comparison of the mode of female education in the last age with the present.

To return, however, to the subject of general education. A young lady may excel in speaking French and Italian, may repeat a few passages from a volume of extracts ; play like a professor, and sing like a syren ; have her dressing-room decorated with her own drawings, tables, stands, flower-pots, screens, and cabinets; nay, she may dance like Sempronia * herself, and yet may have been very badly educated. I am far from meaning to set no value whatever on any or all of these qualifications ; they are all of them elegant, and many of them properly tend to the per-

* See Cataline's Conspiracy.

fecting

fecting of a polite education. Thefe things in their meafure and degree, may be done, but there are others which fhould not be left undone. Many things are becoming, but " one thing is needful." Befides, as the world feems to be fully apprized of the value of whatever tends to embellifh life, there is lefs occafion here to infift on its importance.

But, though a well-bred young lady may lawfully learn moft of the fafhionable arts, yet it does not feem to be the true end of education to make women of fafhion *dancers, fingers, players, painters, actreffes, fculptors, gilders, varnifhers, engravers,* and *embroiderers.* Moft *men* are commonly deftined to fome profeffion, and their minds are confequently turned each to its refpective object. Would it not be ftrange if they were called out to exercife their profeffion, or to fet up their trade, with only a little general knowledge of the trades of all other men, and without any previous definite application to

their

their own peculiar calling ?. The profession of ladies, to which the bent of *their* inftruction fhould be turned, is that of daughters, wives, mothers, and miftreffes of families. They fhould be therefore trained with a view to thefe feveral conditions, and be furnifhed with a ftock of ideas, and principles, and qualifications, and habits, ready to be applied and appropriated, as occafion may demand, to each of thefe refpective fituations : for though the arts which merely embellifh life muft claim admiration; yet when a man of fenfe comes to marry, it is a companion whom he wants and not an artift. It is not merely a creature who can paint, and play, and drefs, and dance ; it is a being who can comfort and counfel him ; one who can reafon, and reflect, and feel, and judge, and act, and difcourfe, and difcriminate ; one who can affift him in his affairs, lighten his cares, foothe his forrows, purify his joys, ftrengthen his principles, and educate his children.

Almoft

Almoſt any ornamental talent is a good thing, when it is not the beſt thing a woman has; and talents are admirable when not made to ſtand proxy for virtues. The writer of theſe pages is intimately acquainted with ſeveral ladies who, excelling moſt of their ſex in the art of muſic, but excelling them alſo in prudence and piety, find little leiſure or temptation, amidſt the delights and duties of a large and lovely family, for the exerciſe of this talent, and regret that ſo much of their own youth was waſted in acquiring an art which can be turned to ſo little account in married life; and are now conſcientiouſly reſtricting their daughters in the portion of time allotted to its acquiſition.

Far be it from me to diſcourage the cultivation of any exiſting talent; but may it not be queſtioned of the fond believing mother, whether talents, like the ſpirits of owen Glendower, though conjured by parental

parental partiality with ever fo loud a
voice,

Yet will they come when you do call for them?

That injudicious practice, therefore,
cannot be too much difcouraged, of endeavouring to create talents which do not
exift in nature. *That their daughters
fhall learn every thing*, is fo general a
maternal maxim, that even unborn daughters, of whofe expected abilities and con-
jectured faculties, it is prefumed, no very
accurate judgment can previoufly be
formed, are yet predeftined to this univerfality of accomplifhments. This com-
prehenfive maxim, thus almoft univerfally
brought into practice, at once weakens
the general powers of the mind, by drawing off its ftrength into too great a variety
of directions; and cuts up time into
too many portions, by fplitting it into fuch
an endlefs multiplicity of employments.
I know that I am treading on tender
ground; but I cannot help thinking that

15   the

the reftlefs pains we take to cram up
every little vacuity of life, by crowding
one new thing upon another, rather
creates a thirſt for novelty than knowledge; and is but a well-difguifed con-
trivance to keep us in after-life more
effectually from converfing with ourfelves.
The care taken to prevent *ennui* is but
a creditable plan for promoting felf-igno-
rance. We run from one occupation to
another, (I fpeak of thofe arts to which
little intellect is applied,) with a view
to lighten the preffure of time; above
all, we fly to them to fave us from our own
thoughts; whereas were we thrown a
little more on our own hands, we might
at laft be driven, by way of fomething to
do, to try to get acquainted with our own
hearts; and though our being lefs abforbed
by this bufy trifling, which dignifies its in-
anity with the impofing name of occupation,
might render us fomewhat more fenfible
of the tedium of life; yet might not this
very fenfation tend to quicken our purfuit
of

Don't they enrich our thoughts?

of a better? For an awful thought here fuggeits itfelf. If life be fo long that we are driven to fet at work every engine to pafs away the tedioufnefs of time; how fhall we do to get rid of the tedioufnefs of eternity? an eternity in which not one of the acquifitions which life has been ex-haulted in acquiring, will be of the leaft ufe? Let not then the foul be ftarved by feeding it on fuch unfubftantial aliment, for it can be no more nourifhed by thefe empty hufks than the body can be fed with ideas and principles.

Among the boafted improvements of the prefent age, none affords more fre-quent matter of peculiar exultation, than the manifeft fuperiority in the employ-ments of the young ladies of our time over thofe of the good houfewives of the *(1700s)* laft century. It is matter of triumph, that they are at prefent employed in learning the polite arts, or in acquiring liberal ac-complifhments; while the others wore out their joylefs days in adorning the manfion-

houfe

houfe with hangings of hideous tapeftry and disfiguring tent-ftitch. Moft chearfully do I allow to the reigning modes their boafted fuperiority; for certainly there is no piety in bad tafte. Still, granting all the deformity of the exploded ornaments, one advantage attended them : the walls and floors were not vain of their decorations; and it is to be feared, that the little perfon fometimes is. The flattery beftowed on the obfolete employments, for probably even *they* had their flatterers, furnifhed lefs aliment and lefs gratification to vanity, and was lefs likely to impair the delicacy and modefty of the fex than the exquifite cultivation of perfonal accomplifhments or perfonal decorations; and every mode which keeps down vanity and keeps back *felf*, has at leaft a moral ufe. And while one admires the elegant fingers of a young lady, bufied in working or painting her ball drefs, one cannot help fufpecting that her alacrity may be a little ftimulated by the animating idea *how very well fhe fhall look*

in

in it. Nor was the induftrious matron of Ithaca more foothed at her folitary loom with the fweet reflection that by her labour fhe was gratifying her filial and conjugal feelings, than the pleafure-loving damfel of Britain, by the anticipated admiration which her ingenuity is procuring for her beauty.

Might not this propenfity be a little checked, and an interefting feeling combined with her induftry, were the fair artift habituated to exercife her fkill in adorning fome one elfe rather than herfelf? For it will add no lightnefs to the lighteft head, nor vanity to the vaineft heart, to take pleafure in reflecting how exceedingly the gown fhe is working will become her mother. This fuggeftion, trifling as it may feem, of habituating young ladies to exercife their tafte and devote their leifure, not to the decoration of their own perfons, but to the fer- *(service)* vice of thofe to whom they are bound by every tender tie, would not only help to reprefs vanity, but by thus affociating the idea of induftry with that of filial affection, would promote, while it gratified fome of the beft affections of the heart. The Romans (and it is mortifying on the fubject of Chriftian education to be driven fo often to refer to the fuperiority of Pagans) were fo well aware of the importance of keeping up a fenfe of family fondnefs and attachment by the very fame means which promoted fimple and domeftic employment, that no citizen of note ever appeared in public in any garb but what was fpun by his wife and daughter; and this virtuous fafhion was not confined to the days of republican feverity, but even in all the pomp and luxury of imperial power, Auguftus preferved in his own family this fimplicity of manners.

Let me be allowed to repeat, that I mean not with prepofterous praife to defcant on the ignorance or the prejudices of paft times, nor abfurdly to regret that vulgar fyftem of education which rounded

the

the little circle of female acquirements within the limits of the fampler and the receipt-book. Yet if a preference almoft exclufive was then given to what was merely ufeful, a preference almoft exclufive alfo is now affigned to what is merely ornamental. And it muft be owned, that if the life of a young lady, formerly, too much refembled the life of a confectioner, it now too much refembles that of an actrefs; the morning is all rehearfal, and the evening is all performance: and thofe who are trained in this regular routine, who are inftructed in order to be exhibited, foon learn to feel a fort of impatience in thofe focieties in which *their* kind of talents are not likely to be brought into play; the tafk of an auditor becomes dull to her who has been ufed to be a performer. Efteem and kindnefs become but cold fubftitutes to her who has been pampered with plaudits and acclamations. And the exceffive commendation which the vifitor is expected to pay for his entertain-

I 2   ment

ment not only keeps alive the flame of
vanity in the artift by conftant fuel, but
is not feldom exacted at a price which a
veracity at all ftrict would grudge; but
when a whole circle are obliged to be competitors who fhall flatter moft, it is not
eafy to be at once very fincere and very
civil. And unluckily, while the age is
become fo knowing and fo faftidious, that
if a young lady does not play like a public
performer, no one thinks her worth attend-
ing to; yet if fhe does fo excel, fome of the
fobereft of the admiring circle feel a ftrong
alloy to their pleafure, on reflecting at what
a vaft expence of time this perfection muft
probably have been acquired *.

* That accurate judge of the human heat,
Madame de Maintenon, was fo well aware of the
danger refulting from fome kinds of excellence, that
after the young ladies of the Court of Louis Quatorze
had diftinguifhed themfelves by the performance of
fome dramatic pieces of Racine, when her friends
told her how admirably they had played their parts;
" Yes," anfwered this wife woman, " fo admirably
" that they fhall never play again."

9   The

The ſtudy of the fine arts indeed is forced on young perſons, with or without genius, (faſhion as was ſaid before having ſwallowed up that diſtinction,) to ſuch exceſs, as to vex, fatigue, and diſguſt thoſe who have no talents, and to determine them, as ſoon as they become free agents, to abandon all ſuch tormenting acquire-ments. While by this inceſſant purſuit ſtill more pernicious effects are often pro-duced on thoſe who actually poſſeſs genius; for the natural conſtant reference to that public performance for which they are ſe-dulouſly cultivating this talent, excites the ſame paſſions of envy, vanity, and compe-tition in the dilettanti performers, as might be ſuppoſed to ſtimulate profeſſional can-didates for fame and profit at public games and theatrical exhibitions. Is this emu-lation, is this ſpirit of rivalry the temper which prudent parents would wiſh to ex-cite and foſter? Beſides, in *any* event the iſſue is not favourable : if the young per-formers are timid, they diſgrace themſelves

I 3   and

and diſtreſs their friends; if courageous, their boldneſs offends ſtill more than their bad performance. Shall they then be ſtudiouſly brought into ſituations in which failure diſcredits and ſucceſs diſguſts?

May I venture, without being accuſed of pedantry, to conclude this chapter with another reference to Pagan examples? The Hebrews, Egyptians, and Greeks, believed that they could more effectually teach their youth maxims of virtue, by calling in the aid of muſic and poetry; theſe maxims, therefore, they put into verſes, and theſe again were ſet to the moſt popular and ſimple tunes, which the children ſang; thus was their love of goodneſs excited by the very inſtruments of their pleaſure; and the ſenſes, the taſte, and the imagination, as it were, preſſed into the ſervice of religion and morals. Dare I appeal to Chriſtian parents, if theſe arts are commonly uſed by *them,* as ſubſidiary to religion and to a ſyſtem of morals much more worthy of every ingenious aid

and

and affociation, which might tend to recommend them to the youthful mind ? Dare I
appeal to Chriftian parents, whether mufic,
which fills up no trifling portion of their
daughters' time, does not fill it without any
moral end, or even fpecific object ? Nay,
whether fome of the favourite fongs of polifhed focieties are not amatory, are not
Anacreontic, more than quite become the
modeft lips of innocent youth and delicate
beauty ?

CHAP. V.

On the religious employment of time.—
On the manner in which holidays are
paffed. — Selfifhnefs and inconfideration
confidered.—Dangers arifing from the
world.

THERE are many well-difpofed parents
who, while they attend to thefe fafhionable
acquirements, do not neglect to infufe
religious knowledge into the minds of
their children; and having done this are
but too apt to conclude that they have
fully acquitted themfelves of the important
duties of education. For having, as they
think, fufficiently grounded them in religion, they do not fcruple to allow their
daughters to fpend almoft the whole of
their time exactly like the daughters
of worldly people. Now, though it be
one great point gained, to have imbued

their

their young minds with the beft knowledge, the work is not therefore by any
means accomplifhed.   " What do ye more
" than others ?" is a queftion which, in a
more extended fenfe, religious parents muft
be prepared to anfwer.

Such parents fhould go on to teach
children the religious ufe of time, the duty
of confecrating to God every talent, every
faculty, every poffeffion, and of devoting
their whole lives to his glory.   People of
piety fhould be more peculiarly on their
guard againft a fpirit of idlenefs, and a
flovenly habitual wafting of time, becaufe
this practice, by not affuming a palpable
fhape of guilt, carries little alarm to
the confcience.   Even religious characters
are in danger on this fide ; for not allowing themfelves to follow the world in
its exceffes and diverfions, they have confequently more time upon their hands; and
inftead of dedicating the time fo refcued
to its true purpofes, they fometimes make
as it were compenfation to themfelves for
                                        their

their abſtinence from dangerous places of
public reſort, by an habitual frivolouſneſs at
home; by a ſuperabundance of unprofitable
ſmall-talk, idle reading, and a quiet and dull
frittering away of time. Their day perhaps
has been more free from actual evil; but it
will often be found to have been as un-
productive as that of more worldly characters; and they will be found to have
traded to as little purpoſe with their
maſter's talents. But a Chriſtian muſt
take care to keep his conſcience peculiarly
alive to the unapparent, though formidable perils of unprofitableneſs.

To theſe, and to all, the author would
earneſtly recommend to accuſtom their
children to paſs at once from ſerious buſineſs to active, and animated recreation;
they ſhould carefully preſerve them from
thoſe long and torpid intervals between
both, that languid indolence and ſpiritleſs
trifling, which wears out ſuch large
portions of life in both young and old.
It has indeed paſſed into an aphoriſm,
that

that activity is neceffary to virtue, even among thofe who are not apprized that it is alfo indifpenfable to happinefs. So far are many parents from being fenfible of this truth, that vacations from fchool are not merely allowed, but appointed to pafs away in wearifome fauntering and indeterminate idlenefs, and this by way of converting the holidays into pleafure! Nay, the idlenefs is fpecifically made over to the child's mind, as the ftrongeft expreffion of the fondnefs of the parent! A diflike to learning is thus fyftematically excited by prepofteroufly erecting indolence into a reward for application! And the promife of doing nothing is held out as the beft recompence for having done well!

These and fuch like errors of conduct arife from the latent but very operative principle of felfifhnefs. This principle is obvioufly promoted by many habits and practices feemingly of little importance; and indeed felfifhnefs is fo commonly

interwoven

interwoven with vanity and inconfideration, that I have not always thought it neceffary to mark the diftinction. They are alternately caufe and effect; and are produced and re-produced by reciprocal operation. They are a joint confederacy who are mutually promoting each other's ftrength and intereft. Ill-judging tendernefs is in fact only a concealed felf-love, which cannot bear to be witnefs to the uneafinefs which a prefent difappointment, or difficulty, or vexation, would caufe to a darling child, yet does not fcruple by improper gratification to ftore up for it future miferies, which the child will infallibly fuffer, though it may be at a diftant period which the mother will be faved the pain of beholding.

Another principle fomething different from this, though it may properly fall under the head of felfifhnefs, feems to actuate fome parents in their conduct towards their children: I mean, a certain flothfulnefs of mind, a love of eafe, which impofes a voluntary blindnefs, and makes
them

them not choofe to fee what will give them trouble to combat. From the perfons in queftion we frequently hear fuch expref-fions as thefe : " Children will be chil-" dren:"—" My children I fuppofe are ·" much like thofe of other people," &c. Thus we may obferve this dangerous and delufive principle frequently turning off with a fmile from the firft indications of thofe tempers, which from their fatal ten-dency ought to be very ferioufly taken up. I would be underftood now as fpeaking to confcientious parents, who confider it as a duty to correct the faults of their children, but who, from this indolence of mind, are extremely backward in *difcovering* fuch faults, and not very well pleafed when they are pointed out by others. Such parents will do well to take notice that whatever they confider it as a duty to *correct*, muft be equally a duty to en-deavour to *find out*. And this love of eafe is the more to be guarded againft, as it not only leads parents into erroneous conduct

conduct towards their children, but is
peculiarly dangerous to themfelves.   It
is a fault frequently cherifhed from ignorance of its real character; for, not
bearing on it the ftrong features of deformity which mark many other vices,
but on the contrary bearing fome refemblance to virtue, it is frequently
miftaken for the Chriftian graces of patience, meeknefs, and forbearance, than
which nothing can be more oppofite;
thefe proceeding from the Chriftian principle of felf-denial, the other from felf-
indulgence.

In this connection may I be permitted
to remark on the practice at the tables
of many families when the children are at
home for the holidays; every delicacy
is forced upon them, with the tempting
remark, " that they cannot have this
" or that dainty at fchool;" and they are
indulged in irregular hours for the fame
motive, " becaufe they cannot have that
" indulgence at fchool." Thus the natural feeds of idlenefs, fenfuality, and
floth,

floth, are at once cherifhed, by converting
the periodical vifit at home into a feafon of
intemperance, late hours, and exemption
from ftudy ; fo that children are habituated, at an age when lafting affociations
are formed in the mind, to connect the
idea of ftudy with that of hardfhip, of happinefs with gluttony, and of pleafure with
loitering, feafting, or fleeping. Would it
not be better to make them combine the
delightful idea of home, with the gratification of the focial affections, the fondnefs
of maternal love, the kindnefs, and warmth,
and confidence of the fweet domeftic attachments,

> ——And all the charities
> Of father, fon, and brother?

I will venture to fay, that thofe liftlefs
and vacant days, when the thoughts have
no precife object; when the imagination
has nothing to fhape; when induftry has no
definite purfuit ; when the mind and the
body have no exercife, and the ingenuity
no acquifition either to anticipate or to

enjoy,

enjoy, are the longeſt, the dulleſt, and the leaſt happy, which children of ſpirit and genius ever paſs. Yes! it is a few ſhort but keen and lively intervals of animated pleaſure, ſnatched from between the ſucceſſive labours and duties of a buſy day, looked forward to with hope, enjoyed with taſte, and recollected without remorſe, which, both to men and to children, yield the trueſt portions of enjoyment. O ſnatch your offspring from adding to the number of thoſe objects of ſupreme commiſeration, who ſeek their happineſs in doing nothing! Life is but a ſhort day; but it is a working day. Activity *may* lead to evil; but inactivity *cannot* be led to good.

Young ladies ſhould alſo be accuſtomed to ſet apart a fixed portion of their time, as ſacred to the poor *, whether in relieving,

I agree with this.

* It would be a noble employment, and well becoming the tenderneſs of their ſex, if ladies were to conſider the ſuperintendance of the poor as their immediate office. They are peculiarly fitted for it; for

lieving, inſtructing, or working for them;
and the performance of this duty muſt
not be left to the event of contingent
circumſtances, or the operation of acci-
dental impreſſions; but it muſt be eſta-
bliſhed into a principle, and wrought into
a habit. A ſpecific portion of time muſt
be allotted to it, on which no common
engagement muſt be allowed to intrench.
This will help to furniſh a powerful
remedy for that ſelfiſhneſs whoſe ſtrong
holds, the truth cannot be too often

---

for from their own habits of life they-are more
intimately acquainted with domeſtic wants than
the other ſex ; and in certain inſtances of ſickneſs and
ſuffering peculiar to themſelves, they ſhould be
expected to have more ſympathy; and they have
obviouſly more leiſure. There is a certain religious
ſociety, diſtinguiſhed by the ſimplicity of their dreſs,
manners, and language, whoſe poor are perhaps
better taken care of than any other ; and one reaſon
may be, that they are immediately under the inſpec-
tion of the women.

repeated.

repeated, it is the grand bufinefs of Chriftian education perpetually to attack. If we were but aware how much better it makes ourfelves to wifh to fee others better, and to affift in making them fo, we fhould find that the good done would be of as much importance by the habit it would induce in our own minds, as by its beneficial effects on others *.

In what relates to pecuniary bounty, it will be requiring of children a very fmall facrifice, if you teach them merely to give that money to the poor which properly belongs to the parent; this fort of charity commonly fubtracts little from

---

* In addition to the inftruction of the individual poor, and the fuperintendance of charity fchools, ladies might be highly ufeful in affifting the parochial clergy in the adoption of that excellent plan for the inftruction of the ignorant fuggefted by the Bifhop of Durham in his laft admirable charge to his clergy. It is with pleafure the author is enabled to add that the fcheme has actually been adopted with good effect in that extenfive diocefe.

their

their own pleafures, efpecially when what they have beftowed is immediately made up to them, as a reward for their little fit of generofity. They will, on this plan, foon learn to give, not only for praife but for profit. The facrifice of an orange to a little girl, or a feather to a great one, given at the expence of their own gratification, would be a better leffon of charity on its right ground, than a confiderable fum of money to be prefently replaced by the parent. And it would be habituating them early to combine two ideas which ought never to be feparated, charity and felf-denial.

As an antidote to felfifhnefs, as well as pride and indolence, they fhould alfo very early be taught to perform all the little offices in their power for themfelves; not to be infolently calling for fervants where there is no real occafion; above all, they fhould be accuftomed to confider the domeftics' hours of meals and reft as almoft facred, and the golden rule fhould

be

be practically and uniformly enforced, even on so trifling an occasion as ringing a bell through mere wantonnefs, or felf-love, or pride.

To check the growth of inconfiderate-nefs, young ladies fhould early be taught to difcharge their little debts with punctuality. They fhould be made fenfible of the cruelty of obliging trades-people to call often for the money due to them; and of hindering and detaining thofe whofe time is the fource of their fubfiftence, under pretence of fome frivolous engagement, which ought to be made to bend to the comfort and advantage of others. They fhould confcientioufly allow fufficient time for the execution of their orders; and with a Chriftian circumfpection, be careful not to drive work-people, by needlefs hurry, into lofing their reft, or breaking the Sabbath. I have known a lady give her gown to a mantua-maker on the Saturday night, to whom fhe would not for the world fay in fo many words,

" You

" You muft work through the whole
" of Sunday," while fhe was virtually
compelling her to do fo, by an injunction
to bring the gown home finifhed on the
Monday morning, on pain of her dif-
pleafure. To thefe hardfhips numbers are
continually driven by good-natured but
inconfiderate employers.   As thefe petty
exactions of inconfideration furnifh alfo
a conftant aliment to felfifhnefs, let not
a defire to counteract them be confidered
as leading to too minute details ; nothing
is too frivolous for animadverfion, which
tends to fix a bad habit in the fuperior, or to wound the feelings of the de-
pendant.

Would it not be turning thofe political
doctrines, which are now fo warmly
agitating, to a truly moral account, and
give the beft practical anfwer to the
popular declamations on the inequality of
human conditions, were the rich carefully to inftruct their children. to foften
that inevitable inequality by the mildnefs
and

and tendernefs of their behaviour to their inferiors? This difpenfation of God, which excites fo many murmurs, would, were it thus practically improved, tend to eftablifh the glory of that Being who is now fo often reviled for his injuftice; for God himfelf is covertly attacked in many of the invectives againft laws and governments, and the fuppofed unjuft difproportion of ranks.

This difpenfation, thus properly improved, would at once call into exercife the generofity, kindnefs, and forbearance of the fuperior; and the patience, refignation, and gratitude of the inferior: and thus, while we were vindicating the *ways* of Providence, we fhould be accomplifhing his *plan*, by bringing into action thofe virtues of both claffes which would have had little exercife had there been no inequality in fortune. Thofe who are fo zealoufly contending for the privileges of rank and power, fhould never lofe fight of the religious duties and confiderate virtues which the poffeffion of rank and

power

Those of "rank and fortune" have a duty to uphold Christian virtues (chapter 1).

THE EMPLOYMENT OF TIME.   135

power impoſes on themſelves ; duties and virtues which ſhould ever be inſeparable from thoſe privileges   As the inferior claſſes have little real right to complain of *laws*, in this reſpect let the great be watchful to give them as little cauſe to complain or *manners.*   In order to this, let them carefully train up their children to ſupply by individual kindneſs thoſe caſes of hardſhip which laws cannot reach ; let them obviate, by an active and well-directed compaſſion, thoſe imperfections of which the beſt conſtructed human inſtitutions muſt unavoidably partake ; and, by the exerciſe of private bounty, early inculcated, ſoften thoſe diſtreſſes which can never come under the cogniſance of public laws : by ſuch means every leſſon of politics may be converted into a leſſon of piety ; and a ſpirit of condeſcending love might win over ſome, whom a ſpirit of invective will only inflame.

It can never be too often repeated, that one of the great objects of education is the forming of habits. Among the inftances of negligence into which even religioufly difpofed parents and teachers are apt to fall, one is, that they are not fufficiently attentive in finding interefting employment for the Sunday. They do not make a fcruple of fometimes allowing their children to fill up the intervals of public worfhip with their ordinary employments and common fchool exercifes. They are not aware that they are thus training their offspring to an early and a fyftematic profanation of the Sabbath by this habit ; for to children, their tafks are their bufinefs ; to them a French or Latin exercife is as ferious an occupation as the exercife of a trade or profeffion is to a man; and if they are allowed to think the one right *now*, they will not be brought hereafter to think that the other is wrong ; for the opinions and practices fixed at this early feafon are not eafily altered. By this overfight even the friends of religion may be contributing

eventually

eventually to that abolition of the Lord's
day, fo devou ly wifhed by its enemies, as
the defired preliminary to the deftruction
of whatever is moft dear to Chriftians.
What obftruction would it offer to the
general progrefs of youth, if all their Sunday exercifes (which, with reading, com-
pofing, tranfcribing, and getting by heart,
might be extended to an entertaining
variety) were adapted to the peculiar nature of the day? It is not meant to impofe
on them fuch rigorous ftudy as fhall convert
the day they fhould be taught to love into
a day of burdens and hardfhips, or to
abridge their innocent enjoyments; but
it is intended merely to fuggeft that there
fhould be a marked diftinction in the
nature of their employments and ftudies;
for on the obfervance or neglect of this,
as was before obferved, their future notions
and principles will in a good degree
be formed. The Gofpel, in refcuing the
Lord's day from the rigorous bondage
of the Jewifh Sabbath, never leffened the
obligation

obligation to keep it holy, nor meant to
fanction any fecular occupation.

Though the author, chiefly writing with
a view to domeftic inftruction, has purpofely avoided entering on the difputed
queftion, whether a fchool or home education be beft; a queftion which perhaps
muft generally be decided by the ftate
of the individual home, and the ftate
of the individual fchool; yet fhe begs leave
to fuggeft one remark, which peculiarly
belongs to a fchool education; namely,
the general habit of converting the Sunday
into a vifiting day by way of gaining time;
as if the appropriate inftru ions of the
Sunday were the cheapeft facrifice which
could be made to pleafure. Even in thofe
fchools, in which religion is confidered as
an indifpenfable part of inftruction, this
kind of inftruction is almoft exclufively
limited to Sundays: how then are girls
ever to make any progrefs in this moft
important article, if they are habituated to
lofe the religious advantages of the fchool,

for

for the fake of having more dainties for dinner abroad? This remark cannot be fuppofed to apply to the vifits which children make to religious parents, and indeed it only applies to thofe cafes where the fchool is a confcientious fchool, and the vifit a trifling vifit.

Among other fubjects which engrofs a good fhare of worldly converfation, one of the moft attracting is beauty. Many ladies have often a random way of talking rapturoufly on the general importance of beauty, who.are yet prudent enough to be very unwilling to let their own daughters find out they are handfome. Perhaps the contrary courfe might be fafer. If the little liftener were not conftantly hearing that beauty is the beft gift, fhe would not be fo vain from fancy-ing herfelf to be the beft gifted. Be lefs folicitous, therefore, to conceal from her a fecret which with all your watchfulnefs fhe will be fure to find out, without your telling;

telling; but rather feek to lower the
eneral value of beauty in her eftimation.
Ufe your daughter in all things to a
different ftandard from that of the world.
It is not by vulgar people and fervants
only that fhe will be told of her being
pretty. She will be hearing it not only
from gay ladies, but from grave men ; fhe
will be hearing it from the whole world
around her. The antidote to the prefent
danger is not now to be fearched for ; it
muft be already operating ; it muft have
been provided for in the foundation laid in
the general principle fhe had been imbib-
ing, before this particular temptation of
beauty came in queftion. And this general
principle is an habitual indifference to
flattery. She muft have learnt not to be
intoxicated by the praife of the world.
She muft have learnt to eftimate things by
their intrinfic worth, rather than by the
world's eftimation. Speak to her with
particular kindnefs and commendation of
plain but amiable girls ; mention with
compaffion

compaffion fuch as are handfome but ill-educated; fpeak cafually of fome who were once thought pretty but have ceafed to be good; make ufe of the fhortnefs and uncertainty of beauty, as ftrong additional reafons for making that which is little valuable in itfelf, ftill lefs valuable. As it is a *new* idea which is always dangerous, you may thus break the force of this danger by allowing her an early intro-duction to this inevitable knowledge, which would become more interefting, and of courfe more perilous by every additional year: and if you can guard againft that fatal error of letting her fee that fhe is more loved on account of her beauty, her familiarity with the idea may be lefs fatal than its novelty afterwards would prove.

But the great and conftant danger to which young perfons in the higher walks of life are expofed, is the prevailing turn and fpirit of general converfation. Even the children of better families, who

are

are well inftructed when at their ftudies, are yet at other times continually beholding the WORLD fet up in the higheft and moft advantageous point of view. Seeing the world! knowing the world! ftanding well with the world! making a figure in the world! is fpoken of as including the whole fum and fubftance of human advantages. They hear their education almoft exclufively alluded to with reference to the *figure* it will enable them to make in the world. In almoft all companies, they hear all that the world admires fpoken of with admiration; rank flattered, fame coveted, power fought, beauty idolized, money confidered as the one thing needful, and as the atoning fubftitute for the want of all other things; profit held up as the reward of virtue, and worldly eftimation as the juft and higheft prize of lawful ambition; and after the very fpirit of the world has been thus habitually infufed into them all the week, one cannot expect much effect from their being coldly told

now

[Marginalia: Because there are corruptions in the world which might Counteract a Chriftian Education?]

[Marginalia: ct]

now and then on Sundays, that they muſt
not " love the world, nor the things of the
" world." To tell them once in ſeven days
that it is a ſin to gratify an appetite which
you have been whetting and ſtimulating
the preceding ſix, is to require from them
a power of ſelf-control, which our knowledge of the impetuoſity of the paſſions,
eſpecially in early age, ſhould have taught
us is impoſſible.

This is not the place to animadvert on
the uſual miſapplication of the phraſe,
" knowing the world;" which term is
commonly applied, in the way of panegyric, to keen, deſigning, ſelfiſh, ambitious men, who ſtudy mankind in order
to turn it to their own account. But in
the true ſenſe of the expreſſion, the ſenſe
which Chriſtian parents would wiſh to im-
preſs on their children, to know the world;
is to know its emptineſs, its vanity, its futi-
lity, and its wickedneſs. To know it, is to
deſpiſe it; and in this view, an obſcure
Chriſtian in a village may be ſaid to know
the

the world better than a hoary courtier or
wily politician; for how can they be said
to *know* it, who go on to love it, to value
it, to be led captive by its allurements, to
give their foul in exchange for its lying
promifes?

But while fo falfe an eftimate is often
made in fafhionable fociety of the real
value of things; that is, while Chriftianity
does *not* furnifh the ftandard, and human
opinion *does*; while the multiplying our
defires is confidered as a fymptom of
elegance, though to fubdue them is made
the grand criterion of religion; while moderation is beheld as indicating a poornefs
of fpirit, though to that very poverty of
fpirit the higheft promife of the Gofpel
is affigned; while worldly wifdom is
enjoined by worldly friends, in contradiction to that affertion, "that the wifdom
" of the world is foolifhnefs with God;"
while the praife of man is to be anxioufly
fought in oppofition to that affurance,
that "the fear of man worketh a fnare;'
　　　　　　　　　　　　　　　　　while

while thefe things are fo, and that they are fo in a good degree who will deny? may we not venture to affirm that a Chriſtian education, though it be not an impoſſible, is yet a very difficult work?

CHAP. VI.

Filial obedience not the character of the age.
—A comparison with the preceding age
in this respect.—Those who cultivate the
mind advised to study the nature of the
soil.—Unpromising children often make
strong characters.—Teachers too apt to
devote their pains almost exclusively to
children of parts.

Among the real improvements of modern times, and they are not a few, it is to be feared that the growth of filial obedience cannot be included. Who can forbear obferving and regretting in a variety of inftances, that not only fons but daughters have adopted fomething of that fpirit of independence, and difdain of control which characterife the times? And is it not obvious that domeftic manners are not

flightly

flightly tinctured with the hue of public principles? The *rights of man* have been difcuffed, t'll we are fomewhat wearied with the difcuffion. To thefe have been oppofed, with more prefumption than prudence, *the rights of woman*. It follows, according to the natural progreffion of human things, that the next ftage of that irradiation which our enlighteners are pouring in upon us will illuminate the world with grave defcants on the *rights of children*.

This revolutionary fpirit in families fuggefts the remark, that among the faults with which it has been too much the fafhion of recent times to load the memory of the imcomparable Milton, one of the charges brought againft his private cha racter (for with his political character we have here nothing to do) has been, that he was fo fevere a father as to have compelled his daughters, after he was blind, to read aloud to him, for his fole pleafure, Greek and Latin authors of which they did not

underftand

underſtand a word. But this is in fact
nothing more than an inſtance of the
ſtrict domeſtic regulations of the age
in which Milton lived; and ſhould not be
brought forward as a proof of the ſeverity
of his individual temper. Nor indeed
in any caſe ſhould it ever be conſidered as
an hardſhip for an affectionate child to
amuſe an afflicted parent, even though it
ſhould be attended with a heavier ſacrifice
of her own pleaſure than in the preſent
inſtance*.

Is

* In ſpite of this too prevailing ſpirit, and at a time
when, by an inverted ſtate of ſociety, ſacrifices of eaſe
and pleaſure are rather exacted by children from parents, than required of parents from children, numberleſs inſtances might be adduced of filial affection truly
honourable to the preſent period. And the author
records with pleaſure, that ſhe has ſeen amiable young
ladies of high rank conducting the ſteps of a blind
but illuſtrious parent with true filial fondneſs; and
has often contemplated, in another family, the intereſting attentions of daughters who were both hands
and eyes to an infirm and nearly blind father. It is
but

Is the author then inculcating the harſh doctrine of parental auſterity? By no means. It drives the gentle ſpirit to artifice, and the rugged to deſpair. It generates deceit and cunning, the moſt hopeleſs and hateful in the whole catalogue of female failings. Ungoverned anger in the teacher, and inability to diſcriminate between venial errors and premeditated offence, though they may lead a timid creature to hide wrong tempers, or to conceal bad actions, will not help her to ſubdue the one or correct the other. Severity will drive terrified children to ſeek, not for reformation, but for impunity. A readineſs to forgive them promotes frankneſs. And we ſhould, above all things, encourage them to be frank, in order to come at their faults. They have not more

---

but juſtice to add, that theſe examples are not taken from that middle rank of life which Milton filled, but from the daughters of the higheſt officers in the ſtate.

faults

faults for being open, they only *difcovcr* more.

Difcipline, however, is not cruelty, and reftraint is not feverity. We muft ftrengthen the feeble, while we repel the bold. We cannot educate by a *receipt;* for after ftudying the beft rules, and after digefting them into a fyftem, much muft depend on contingent circumftances. The cultivator of the human mind muft, like the gardener, ftudy diverfities of foil, or he may plant diligently and water faithfully with little fruit. The fkilful labourer knows that even where the furface is not particularly promifing, there is often a rough ftrong ground which will amply repay he trouble of breaking it up; yet we are often moft taken with a foft furface, though it conceal a fhallow depth, becaufe it promifes prefent reward and little trouble. But ftrong and pertinacious tempers, of which perhaps obftinacy is the leading vice, under fkilful management often turn out fteady and fterling charaéters; while from

from fofter clay a firm and vigorous virtue is but feldom produced.

But thefe revolutions in character cannot be effected by mere education. Plutarch has obferved that the medical fcience would never be brought to perfection till poifons fhould be converted into phyfic. What uur late improvers in natural fcience have done in the medical world, by converting the moft deadly ingredients into inftruments of life and health, Chriftianity with a fort of divine alchymy has effected in the moral world, by that tranfmutation which makes thofe paffions which have been working for fin become active in the caufe of religion. The violent temper of Saul of Tarfus, which was " exceedingly " mad" againft the faints of God, did God fee fit to convert into that burning zeal which enabled Paul the Apoftle to labour fo unremittingly for the converfion of the Gentile world. Chriftianity indeed does not fo much give us new affections or fa-

culties.

culties, as give a new direction to thofe we already have. She changes that forrow of the world which worketh death, into " godly forrow which worketh repent- " ance." She changes our anger againft the perfons we diflike into hatred of their fins. " The fear of man which worketh " a fnare," fhe tranfmutes into "·that fear " of God which worketh falvation." That religion does not extinguifh the paffions, but alters their object, the animated ex- preffions of the fervid Apoftle confirm— " Yea, what *fearfulnefs* ; yea, what *clear-* " *ing of yourfelves* ; yea, what *indignation* ; " yea, what *fear* ; yea, what *vehement* " *defire* ; yea, what *zeal* ; yea, what " *revenge* * *!*"

Thus, by fome of the moft troublefome paffions of our nature being converted by the bleffing of God on a religious education to the fide of virtue, a double purpofe is effected. Becaufe, if I may be allowed to change the metaphor, it is the

* 2 Corinthians, vii. 11.

character

character of the paffions never to obferve
a neutrality. If they are no longer rebels,
they become auxiliaries; and a foe fubdued is an ally obtained. And it is the
effect of religion on the paffions, that
when fhe feizes the enemy's garrifon, fhe
does not content herfelf with defeating its
future mifchiefs, fhe does not deftroy the
works, fhe does not burn the arfenal and
fpike the cannon; but the artillery fhe
feizes, fhe turns to her own ufe; fhe attacks in her turn, and plants its whole force
againft the enemy from whom fhe has
taken it.

But while I would deprecate harfhnefs,
I would enforce difcipline; and that not
merely on the ground of religion, but
of happinefs alfo. One reafon, not feldom
brought forward by tender but miftaken
mothers as an apology for their unbounded indulgence, efpecially to weakly
children, is, that they probably will not
live to enjoy the world when grown up,
and that therefore they would not abridge
the

the little pleafure they may enjoy at prefent. But a flight degree of obfervation
would prove that this is an error in judgment as well as in principle. For, omitting any confiderations refpecting their
future welfare, and entering only into their
immediate interefts; it is an indifputable
fact that children who know no control,
whofe faults encounter no contradiction,
and whofe humouis experience conftant
indulgence, grow more irritable and capricious, invent wants, create defires, lofe
all relifh for the pleafures which they
know they may reckon upon ; and become
perhaps more miferable than even thofe
unfortunate children who labour under the
more obvious and more commiferated mif-
fortune of fuffering under the tyranny of
unkind parents.

An early habitual reftraint is peculiarly
important to the future character and happinefs of women. A judicious, unrelax-
ing, but fteady and gentle curb on their
tempers and paffions can alone enfure their
peace

peace and eftablifh their principles. It is
a habit which cannot be adopted too foon,
nor perfifted in too pertinacioufly. They
fhould when very young be enured to contradiction. Inftead of hearing their *bon-
mots* treafured up and repeated to the
guefts till they begin to think it dull, when
they themfelves are not the little heroine of
the theme, they fhould be accuftomed to
receive but little praife for their vivacity or
their wit, though they fhould receive juft
commendation for their patience, their
induftry, their humility, and other qualities
which have more worth than fplendour.
They fhould be led to diftruft their own
judgment; they fhould learn not to mur-
mur at expoftulation; but fhould be
accuftomed to expect and to endure oppofition. It is a leffon with which the world
will not fail to furnifh them; and they
will not practife it the worfe for having
learnt it the fooner. It is of the laft importance to their happinefs even in this life
hat they fhould early acquire a fubmiffive
temper

temper and a forbearing fpirit. They muft even endure to be thought wrong fometimes, when they cannot but feel they are right. And while they fhould be anxioufly afpiring to do well, they muft not expect always to obtain the praife of having done fo. But while a gentle demeanor is inculcated, let them not be inftructed to practife gentlenefs merely on the low ground of its being decorous, and feminine, and pleafing, and calculated to attract human favour : but let them be carefully taught to cultivate it on the high principle of obedience to Chrift; on the practical ground of labouring after conformity to HIM, who, when he propofed himfelf as a perfect pattern of imitation, did not fay, Learn of me, for I am great, or wife, or mighty, but " Learn of me, for I " am meek and lowly :" and gracioufly promifed that the reward fhould accompany the practice, by encouragingly adding, " and ye fhall find reft to your fouls." Do not teach them humility on the ordinary

nary ground that vanity is *unamiable*, and that no one will *love* them if they are proud ; for that will only go to correct the exterior, and make them foft and fmiling hypocrites. But inform them, that " God " refifteth the proud," while " them " that are meek he fhall guide in judg- " ment, and fuch as are gentle, them fhall " he teach his way." In thefe, as in all other cafes, an habitual attention to the *motives* fhould be carefully fubftituted in their young hearts, in the place of too much anxiety about the *event* of actions. Principles, aims, and intentions fhould be invariably infifted on, as the only true ground of right practice, and they fhould be carefully guarded againft too much folicitude for that human praife which attaches to appearances as much as to realities, to fuccefs more than to defert.

Let me repeat, that it will be of vaft importance not to let flip the earlieft occafions of working gentle manners into an habit on their only true foundation, Chriftian

meek-

meeknefs. For this purpofe I would again
urge your calling in the example of our
Redeemer in aid of his precepts. Endeavour to make your pupil feel that all the
wonders exhibited in his life do not fo
overwhelm the awakened heart with rapture, love, and aftoni hment, as the perpetual inftances of his humility and meeknefs. Stupendous miracles, exercifes of
infinite power prompted by infinite mercy,
are actions which we fhould naturally
enough conceive as growing out of the
divine perfections: but filence under
cruel mockings, patience under reproach,
gentlenefs of demeanor under unparalleled
injuries; thefe are perfections of which
unaffifted nature not only has no conception in a Divine Being, but at which it
would revolt, had not the reality been
exemplified by our perfect pattern. Heal-
ing the fick, feeding the multitude, reftor-
ing the blind, raifing the dead, are deeds
of which we could form fome adequate
idea, as neceffarily flowing from Almighty
good

goodnefs : but to wafh his difciples' feet, —to preach the Gofpel to the *poor*,—to renounce not only eafe, for that heroes have done on human motives,—but to renounce praife, to forgive his perfecutors, to love his enemies, to pray for his murderers with his laft breath;—thefe are things which, while they compel us to cry out with the Centurion, " Truly " this was the Son of God," fhould remind us alfo, that they are not only *adorable* but *imitable* parts of his character. Thefe are perfections which we are not barely to contemplate with holy awe and diftant admiration, as if they were reftricted to the *divine* nature of our Redeemer ; but we muft confider them as fuited to the human nature alfo, which he condefcended to participate ; in *contemplating*, we muft *imitate* ; in admiring, we muft practife ; and in our meafure and degree go and do likewife. Elevate your thoughts for one moment to this ftandard, (and never allow yourfelf to be contented

with

with a lower,) and then go, if you can, and teach your children to be mild, and foft, and gentle on worldly grounds, on human motives, and as an external attraction.

There is a cuftom among teachers, which is not the more right for being common; they are apt to beftow an undue proportion of pains on children of the beft capacity, as if only geniufes were worthy of attention. They fhould reflect that in moderate talents, carefully cultivated, we are perhaps to look for the chief happinefs and virtue of fociety. If fuperlative genius had been generally neceffary, its exiftence would not have been fo rare; for Omnipotence could eafily have made thofe talents common which we now confider as extraordinary had they been neceffary to the perfection of his plan. Befides, while we are confcientioufly inftructing children of moderate capacity, it is a comfort to reflect, that if no labour will raife them to a high degree in the fcale

of

of intellectual excellence, yet they may be led on to perfection in that road in which " a way-faring man, though simple, shall " not err." And when a mother feels disposed to repine that her family is not likely to exhibit a groupe of future wits and growing beauties, let her console herself by looking abroad into the world, where she will quickly perceive that the monopoly of happiness is not engrossed by beauty, nor that of virtue by genius.

Perhaps mediocrity of parts was decreed to be the ordinary lot, by way of furnishing a stimulus to industry, and strengthening the motives to virtuous application. For is it not obvious that moderate abilities, carefully carried to that measure of perfection of which they are capable, often enable their possessors to outstrip, in the race of knowledge and of usefulness, their more brilliant but less persevering competitors? It is with mental endowments, as with other rich gifts of Providence; the inhabitant of the luxuriant fouthern clime, where Nature has done every thing in the way of vegetation, indolently lays hold on this very fertility as a plea for doing nothing himfelf; fo that the foil which teems with fuch encouraging abundance leaves the favoured poffeffor idle; while the native of the lefs genial region, fupplying by his labours the deficiencies of his lot, overtakes his more favoured competitor; by fubftituting induftry for opulence, he improves the riches of his native land beyond that which is bleffed with warmer funs, and thus vindicates Providence from the charge of partial diftribution.

A girl who has docility will feldom be found to want underftanding fufficient for all the purpofes of a ufeful, a happy, and a pious life. And it is as wrong for parents to fet out with too fanguine a dependence on the figure their children are to make in life, as it is unreafonable to be difcouraged at every difappointment. Want of fuccefs is fo far from furnifhing a
motive

motive for relaxing their energy, that it is a reafon for redoubling it. Let them fufpect their own plans, and reform them; let them diftruft their own principles, and correct them. The generality of parents do too little; fome do much, and mifs their reward, becaufe they look not to any ftrength beyond their own : after much is done, much will remain undone; for the entire regulation of the heart and affections is not the work of education alone, but the operation of divine grace. Will it be accounted enthufiafm to fuggeft, "that " the fervent effectual prayer of a " righteous *parent* availeth much?" and perhaps the reafon why fo many anxious mothers fail of fuccefs is, becaufe they repofe with confidence in their own fkill and labour, without looking to HIM without whofe blelfing they do but labour in vain.

On the other hand, is it not to be feared that fome pious parents have fallen into an error of an oppofite kind? From a

full

full conviction that human endeavours are
vain, and that it is God alone who can
change the heart, they are earneſt in their
prayers, but not ſo earneſt in their endeavours. Such parents ſhould be re-
minded, that if they do not add their
exertions to their prayers, their children
are not likely to be more benefited than
the children of thoſe who do not add their
prayers to their exertions. What God
has joined, let not man preſume to ſeparate. It *is* the work of God, we readily
acknowledge, to implant religion in the
heart, and to maintain it there as a ruling
principle of conduct. And is it not the
ſame God which cauſes the corn to grow?
Are not our natural lives conſtantly preſerved by his power? Who will deny
that in him we live, and move, and have
our being? But how are theſe works
of God carried on? By *means* which he
has appointed. By the labour of the
huſbandman the corn is made to grow:
by food the body is ſuſtained: and by
religious

religious inftruction God is pleafed to work
upon the human heart. As far as *we* fee
of the ways of God, all his works are
carried on by *means*. It becomes therefore our duty to ufe the means, and truft
in God; to remember that God will not
work without the means; and that the
means can effect nothing without his blefling. " Paul may plant and Apollos water,
" but it is God muft give the increafe."
But to what does he give the increafe?
To the *exertions* of Paul and Apollos.
It is never faid, becaufe God only can
give the increafe, that Paul and Apollos
may fpare their labour.

It is one grand object to give the young
probationer juft and fober views of the
world on which fhe is about to enter.
Inftead of making her bofom bound at the
near profpect of emancipation from her
inftructors; inftead of teaching her young
heart to dance with premature flutterings
as the critical winter draws near in which
fhe is to come out; inftead of raifing a
tumult

tumult in her bufy imagination at the approach of her firft *grown up ball;* endeavour
to convince her, that the world will not
turn out to be that fcene of unvarying and
never-ending delights which fhe has perhaps been led to expect, not only from the
fanguine temper and warm fpirits natural
to youth, but from the value fhe has feen
put on thofe fhowy accomplifhments which
have too probably been fitting her for
her exhibition in life. Teach her that
this world is not a ftage for the difplay
of fuperficial or even of fhining talents,
but for the ftrict and fober exercife of fortitude, temperance, meeknefs, faith, diligence, and felf-denial; of her due performance of which Chriftian graces
Angels will be fpectators, and God th
judge. Teach her that human life is not
a fplendid romance, fpangled over with
brilliant adventures, and enriched with
extraordinary occurrences, and diverfified
with wonderful incidents; lead her not to
expect that it will abound with fcenes
                                    which

which will call shining qualities and great powers into perpetual action; and for which if she acquit herself well she will be rewarded with proportionate fame and certain commendation. But apprize her that human life is a true history, many passages of which will be dull, obscure, and uninteresting; some perhaps tragical; but that whatever gay incidents and pleasing scenes may be interspersed in the progress of the piece, yet finally " one " event happeneth to all ;" to all there is one awful and infallible catastrophe. Apprize her that the estimation which mankind forms of merit is not always just, nor is its praise exactly proportioned to desert ; that the world weighs actions in far different scales from " the balance of the sanctuary," and estimates worth by a far different standard from that of the gospel : apprize her that while her purest intentions may be sometimes calumniated, and her best actions misrepresented, she will be liable to receive commendation on occasions wherein her

con-

confcience will tell her fhe has not deferved it ; and may be extolled by others for actions for which, if fhe be honeft, fhe may condemn herfelf.

Do not however give her a gloomy and difcouraging picture of the world, but rather feek to give her a juft and fober view of the part fhe will have to act in it. And humble the impetuofity of hope, and cool the ardour of expectation, by explaining to her, that this part, even in her beft eftate. will probably confift in a fucceffion of petty trials, and a round of quiet duties which, however well performed, though they will make little or no figure in the book of Fame, will prove of vaft importance to her in that day when *another* " book is opened, and the judgment is fet, " and every one will be judged according " to the deeds done in the body, whether " they be good or bad."

Say not that thefe juft and fober views will cruelly wither her young hopes, and deaden the innocent fatisfactions of life.

life. It is not true. There is, happily, an active spring in the mind of youth which bounds with fresh vigour and uninjured elasticity from any such temporary depression. It is not meant that you should darken her prospect, so much as that you should enlighten her understanding to contemplate it. And though her feelings, tastes, and passions, will all be against you, if you set before her a faithful delineation of life, yet it will be something to get her judgment on your side. It is no unkind office to assist the short view of youth with the aids of long-sighted experience, to enable them to discover spots in the brightness of that life which dazzles them in prospect, though it is probable they will after all choose to believe their own eyes rather than the offered glass.

CHAP. VII

On female· ftudy, and initiation into know-
ledge.—Error of cultivating the imagina-
tion to the neglect of the judgment.—Books
of reafoning recommended.

As this little work by no means affumes
the character of a general fcheme of education, the author has purpofely avoided
expatiating largely on any kind of inftruction; but fo far as it is connected,
either immediately or remotely, with objects of a moral or religious nature. Of
courfe fhe has been fo far from thinking it
neceffary to enter into the enumeration of
thofe books which are ufed in general inftruction, that fhe has purpofely forborne to
mention any. With fuch books the rifing
generation is far more copioufly and ably
furnifhed than any preceding period has
been;

been ; and out of an excellent variety the judicious inftructor can hardly fail to make fuch a felection as fhall be beneficial to the pupil.

But while due praife ought not to be withheld from the improved methods of communicating the elements of general knowledge; yet is there not fome danger that our very advantages may lead us into error, by caufing us to repofe fo confidently on the multiplied helps which facilitate the entrance into learning, as to render our pupils fuperficial through the very facility of acquirement? Where fo much is done for them, may they not be led to do too little for themfelves ? and befides that exertion may flacken for want of a fpur, may there not be a moral difadvantage in poffeffing them with the notion that learning may be acquired without diligence and without labour? Sound education never *can* be made a " primrofe " path of dalliance." Do what we will, we cannot *cheat* children into learning, or

play

play them into knowledge, according to the
smoothnefs of the modern creed, and the
indolence of modern habits.   There is no
idle way to any acquifitions which really
deferve the name.   And as Euclid, in order
to reprefs the impetuous vanity of greatnefs, told his Sovereign that there was no
royal way to geometry, fo the fond mother
may be affured that there is not fhort cut to
any other kind of learning.   The tree of
knowledge, as a punifhment, perhaps, for
its having been at firft unfairly tafted, cannot now be climbed without difficulty ;
and this very circumftance ferves afterwards
to furnifh not only literary pleafures, but
moral advantages : for the knowledge
which is acquired by unwearied affiduity is
lafting in the poffeffion, and fweet to the
poffeffor ; both perhaps in proportion to
the coft and labour of the acquifition.
And though an able teacher ought to
endeavour, by improving the communicating faculty in himfelf, (for many know
what they cannot teach,) to foften every
difficulty ;

difficulty; yet in fpite of the kindnefs and ability with which he will fmooth every obftruction, it is probably among the wife inftitutions of Providence that great difficulties fhould ftill remain. For education is but an initiation into that life of trial to which we are introduced on our entrance into this world. It is the firft breaking-in to that ftate of toil and labour to which we are born, and to which fin has made us liable; and in this view of the fubject the laborious acquifition of learning may be converted to higher ufes than fuch as are purely literary.

Will it not be afcribed to a captious fingularity, if I venture to remark that real knowledge and real piety, though they may have gained in many inftances, have fuffered in others from that profufion of little, amufing, fentimental books with which the youthful library overflows? Abundance has its dangers as well as fcarcity. In the firft place may not the multiplicity of thefe alluring little works
increafe

increafe the natural reluctance to thofe
more dry and uninterefting ftudies, of
which, after all, the rudiments of every
part of learning *muft* confift? And,
fecondly, is there not fome danger (though
there are many honourable exceptions)
that fome of thofe engaging narratives
may ferve to infufe into the youthful heart
a fort of fpurious goodnefs, a confidence of
virtue, a parade of charity? And that the
benevolent actions with the recital of which
they abound, when they are not made to
flow from any fource but feeling, may tend
to infpire a felf-complacency, a felf-gratu-
lation, a " ftand by, for I am holier than
" thou?" May they not help to fuggeft
a falfe ftandard of morals, to infufe a
love of popularity and an anxiety for
praife, in the place of that fimple and
unoftentatious rule of doing whatever good
we do, *becaufe it is the will of God?* The
univerfal fubftitution of this principle
would tend to purify the worldly morality
of many a popular little ftory.   And there
                                         are

are few dangers which good parents will
more carefully guard againſt than that of
giving their children a mere political piety;
that ſort of religion which juſt goes to make
people more reſpectable, and to ſtand well
with the world ; a religion which is to ſave
appearances without inculcating realities, a
religion which affects to " preach peace and
" good-will to men," but which forgets to
give " glory to God on high *."

There is a certain precocity of mind
which is much helped on by theſe ſuperficial modes of inſtruction ; for frivolous
reading will produce its correſpondent
effect, in much leſs time than books

---

* An ingenious (and in many reſpects uſeful)
French Treatiſe on Education, has too much encouraged this political piety; by conſidering religion
as a thing of human convenſion, rather than of
divine inſtitution ; as a thing creditable, rather than
commanded : by erecting the doctrine of expediency
in the place of Chriſtian ſimplicity ; and wearing
away the ſpirit of truth, by the ſubſtitution of occa-
ſional deceit, equivocation, ſubterfuge, and mental
reſervation.

of

of folid inftruction; the imagination being
liable to be worked upon, and the feelings
to be fet a-going, much fafter than the
underftanding can be opened and the
judgment enlightened. A talent for converfation fhould be the refult of education, not its precurfor; it is a golden fruit
when fuffered to ripen gradually on the
tree of knowledge; but if forced in the
hot-bed of a circulating library, it will
turn out worthlefs and vapid in proportion
as it was artificial and premature. Girls
who have been accuftomed to devour
frivolous books, will converfe and write
with a far greater appearance of fkill as
to ftyle and fentiment at twelve or four-
teen years old, than thofe of a more
advanced age who are under the difcipline
of feverer ftudies; but the former having
early attained to that low ftandard which
had been held out to them, become
ftationary; while the latter, quietly pro-
greffive, are paffing through juft gradations
to a higher ftrain of mind; and thofe
who

who early begin with talking and writing like women, commonly end with thinking and acting like children.

The irregular fancy of women is not fufficiently fubdued by early application, nor tamed by labour, and the kind of knowledge they commonly do acquire is eafily attained : and being chiefly an acquifition of the memory, fomething which is given them to get off by themfelves, and not grounded in their minds by comment and converfation, it is eafily loft. The fuperficial *queftion*-and-*anfwer*-way, for inftance, in which they often learn hiftory, furnifhes the mind with little to lean on : the events being detached and feparated, the actions having no links to unite them with each other, the characters not being interweaved by mutual relation, the chronology being reduced to difconnected dates, inftead of prefenting an unbroken feries; of courfe, neither events, actions, characters, nor chronology, faften themfelves on the underftanding, but rather float in the

memory

memory than contribute to form the mind
of the reader, or enrich his judgment in
the important fcience of men and manners.
The fwarms of *Abridgments*, *Beauties*,
and *Compendiums*, which form too confiderable a part of a young lady's library,
may be confidered in many inftances as an
infallible receipt for making a fuperficial
mind. The *names* of the renowned characters in hiftory thus become familiar in
the mouths of thofe who can neither
attach to the ideas of the perfon, the feries
of his actions nor the peculiarities of his
character. A few fine paffages from the
poets (paffages perhaps which derived
their chief beauty from their pofition
and connection) are huddled together by
fome extract-maker, whofe brief and difconnected patches of broken and dif-
cordant materials, while they inflame young
readers with the vanity of reciting, neither
fill the mind nor form the tafte : and it is
not difficult to trace back to their-fhallow
fources the hackney'd quotations of certain

tain *accomplished* young ladies, who will be
frequently found not to have come legiti-
mately by any thing they know : I mean,
not to have drawn it from its true spring,
the original works of the author from
which some *beauty-monger* has severed it.
Human inconsistency in this, as in other
cases, wants to combine two irreconcileable things ; it strives to unite the reputation of knowledge with the pleasures of
idleness, forgetting that nothing that is
valuable can be obtained without sacrifices,
and that if we would purchase knowledge,
we must pay for it the fair and lawful
price of time and industry.   For this
extract-reading, while it accommodates
itself to the convenience, illustrates the
character of the age in which we live.
The appetite for pleasure, and that love of
ease and indolence which is generated by
it, leave little time or taste for sound im-
piovement ; while the vanity, which is
equally a characteristic of the existing
period, puts in its claim also for indul-

N 2   gence,

gence, and contrives to figure away by
thefe little fnatches of reading, caught in
the fhort intervals of fucceffive amufements.
Befides, the tafte, thus pampered with
delicious morfels, is early vitiated. The
young reader of thefe *cluftered beauties*
conceives a difrelifh for every thing which
is plain, and grows impatient if obliged to
get through thofe equally neceffary though
lefs fhowy parts of a work, in which perhaps the author gives the beft proof of his
judgment by keeping under that occafional
brilliancy and incidental ornament, of
which thefe fuperficial ftudents are in conftant purfuit. In all well-written books,
there is much that is good which is not
dazzling; and thefe fhallow critics fhould
be taught, that it is for the embellifhment
of the more tame and uninterefting parts
of his work, that the judicious poet commonly referves thofe flowers, whofe beauty
is defaced when they are plucked from the
garland into which he had fo fkilfully
woven them.

The

The remark, however, as far as it relates to abridgments, is by no means of
general application ; there are many valuable works which from their bulk would
be almoſt inacceſſible to a great number of
readers, and a conſiderable part of which
may not be generally uſeful. Even in the
beſt written books there is often ſuper-
fluous matter; authors are apt to get
enamoured of their ſubjeſt, and to dwell
too long on it : every perſon cannot find
time to read a longer work on any ſubjeſt,
and yet it may be we'l for them to know
ſomething on almoſt every ſubjeſt ; thoſe,
therefore, who abridge voluminous works
judiciouſly, render ſervice to the commu-
nity. But there ſeems, if I may venture
the remark, to be a miſtake in the *uſe* of
abridgments. They are put ſyſtematically
into the hands of *youth*, who have, or
ought to have, leiſure for the works at
large ; while abridgments ſeem more immediately calculated for perſons in more

advanced

advanced life, who wifh to recall fomething they had forgotten ; who want to reftore old ideas rather than acquire new ones; or they are ufeful for perfons immerfed in the bufinefs of the world, who have little leifure for voluminous reading. They are excellent to refrefh the mind, but not competent to form it.

Perhaps there is fome analogy between the mental and bodily conformation of women. The inftructor therefore fhould imitate the phyfician. If the latter prefcribe bracing medicines for a body of which delicacy is the difeafe, the former would do well to prohibit relaxing reading for a mind which is already of too foft a texture, and fhould ftrengthen its feeble tone by invigorating reading.

By foftnefs, I cannot be fuppofed to mean imbecility of underftanding, but natural foftnefs of heart, and pliancy of temper, together with that indolence of fpirit which is foftered by indulging in
feducing

feducing books, and in the general habits of fafhionable life.

I mean not here to recommend books which are immediately religious, but fuch as exercife the reafoning faculties, teach the mind to get acquainted with its own nature, and to ftir up its own powers. Let not a timid young lady ftart if I fhould venture to recommend to her, after a proper courfe of preparation, to fwallow and digeft fuch ftrong meat as Watts's or Duncan's little book of Logic, fome parts of Mr. Locke's Effay on the Human Underftanding, and Bifhop Butler's Analogy. Where there is leifure, and capacity, and an able friend to comment and to counfel, works of this nature might be profitably fubftituted in the place of fo much Englifh Sentiment, French Philofophy, Italian Love-Songs, and fantaftic German imagery and magic wonders. While fuch enervating or abfurd books fadly difqualify the reader for folid purfuit or vigorous thinking, the ftudies here recommended would

act

act upon the conftitution of the mind as a
kind of alterative, and, if I may be allowed
the expreffion, would help to brace the
intellectual ftamina.

This is however by no means intended
to exclude works of tafte and imagination,
which muft always make the ornamental
part, and of courfe a very confiderable
part, of female ftudies. It is only fuggefted, that they fhould not form them
entirely and exclufively. For what is
called dry tough reading, independent
of the knowledge it conveys, is ufeful as
an habit, and wholefome as an exercife.
Serious ftudy ferves to harden the mind
for more trying conflicts; it lifts the reader
from fenfation to intellect; it abftracts
her from the world and its vanities; it
fixes a wandering fpirit, and fortifies a
weak one; it divorces her from matter;
it corrects that fpirit of trifling which fhe
naturally contracts from the frivolous turn
of female converfation, and the petty
nature of female employments; it concen-
trates

trates her attention, affifts her in a habit of
excluding trivial thoughts, and thus even
helps to qualify her for religious purfuits.
Yes, I repeat it, there is to woman a
Chriftian ufe to be made of fober ftudies ;
while books of an oppofite caft, however
unexceptionable they may be fometimes
found in point of expreffion, however free
from evil in its more grofs and palpable
fhapes, yet from their very nature and conftitution they excite a fpirit of relaxation, by
exhibiting fcenes and fuggefting ideas which
foften the mind and fet the fancy at work ;
they take off reftraint, diminifh fober-mind-
ednefs, impair the general powers of refift-
ance, and at beft feed habits of improper
indulgence, and nourifh a vain and vifion-
ary indolence, which lays the mind open
to error and the heart to feduction.

Women are little accuftomed to clofe
reafoning on any fubject ; ftill lefs do they
inure their minds to confider particular
parts of a fubject; they are not habituated
to turn a truth round, and view it in all its

varied

varied afpects and pofitions; and this perhaps is one caufe (as will be obferved
in another * place) of the too great confidence they are difpofed to place in their
own opinions. Though their imagination
is already too lively, and their judgment
naturally incorrect; in educating them we
go on to ftimulate the imagination, while
we neglect the regulation of the judgment.
They already want ballaft, and we make
their education confift in continually
crowding more fail than they can carry.
Their intellectual powers being fo little
ftrengthened by exercife, makes every
little bufinefs appear a hardfhip to them:
whereas ferious ftudy would be ufeful,
were it only that it leads the mind to the
habit of conquering difficulties. But it is
peculiarly hard to turn at once from
the indolent repofe of light reading, from
the concerns of mere animal life, the
objects of fenfe, or the frivoloufnefs of

* Chapter on Converfation.

chit

chit chat; it is peculiarly hard, I fay, to a mind fo foftened, to refcue itfelf from the dominion of felf-indulgence, to refume its powers, to call home its fcattered ftrength, to fhut out every foreign intrufion, to force back a fpring fo unnaturally bent, and to devote itfelf to religious reading, to active bufinefs, to fober reflection, to felf-examination : whereas to an intellect accuftomed to think at all, the difficulty of thinking ferioufly is obvioufly leffened.

Far be it from me to defire to make fcholaftic ladies or female dialecticians ; but there is little fear that the kind of books here recommended, if thoroughly ftudied, and not fuperficially fkimmed, will make them pedants or induce conceit; for by fhewing them the poffible powers of the human mind, you will bring them to fee the littlenefs of their own ; and to get acquainted with the mind, and to regulate and inform it, and to fhew it its own ignorance, does not feem the way to puff it up. But let her who is difpofed to be elated

2   with

with her literary acquifitions, check her
vanity by calling to mind the juft remark
of Swift, "that after all her boafted ac-
" quirements, a woman will, generally
" fpeaking, be found to poffefs lefs of
" what is called learning than a common
" fchool-boy."

Neither is there any fear that this fort of
reading will convert ladies into authors.
The direct contrary effect will be likely to
be produced by the perufal of writers who
throw the generality of readers at fuch an
unapproachable diftance as to check prefumption, inftead of exciting it.   Who are
thofe ever multiplying authors, that with
unparalleled fecundity are overftocking the
world with their quick-fucceeding progeny?
They are NOVEL-WRITERS; the eafinefs of
whofe productions is at once the caufe of
their own fiuitfulnefs, and of the almoft
infinitely numerous race of imitators to
whom they give birth.   Such is the frightful facility of this fpecies of compofition,
that every raw girl, while fhe reads, is
                                    tempted

tempted to fancy that fhe can alfo write.
And as Alexander, on perufing the Iliad,
found by congenial fympathy the image
of Achilles ftamped on his own ardent foul,
and felt himfelf the hero he was ftudying;
and as Corregio, on firft beholding a picture which exhibited the perfection of the
graphic art, prophetically felt all his own
future greatnefs, and cried out in rapture,
" And I too am a painter!" fo a thorough-
paced novel-reading Mifs, at the clofe of
every tiffue of hackney'd adventures, feels
within herfelf the ftirring impulfe of cor-
refponding genius, and triumphantly ex-
claims, " And I too am an author!"
The glutted imagination foon overflows
with the redundance of cheap fentiment
and plentiful incident, and by a fort of
arithmetical proportion, is enabled by the
perufal of any three novels, to produce a
fourth ; till every frefh production, like
the progeny of Banquo, is followed by

> Another, and another, and another!

Is

Is a lady, however deſtitute of talents, education, or knowledge of the world, whoſe ſtudies have been completed by a circulating library, in any diſtreſs of mind? the writing a novel ſuggeſts itſelf as the beſt ſoother of her ſorrows! Does ſhe labour under any depreſſion of circumſtances? writing a novel occurs as the readieſt receipt for mending them! And ſhe ſolaces her imagination with the conviction that the ſubſcription which has been extorted by her importunity, or given to her neceſſities, has been offered as an homage to her genius. And this confidence inſtantly levies a freſh contribution for a ſucceeding work. Capacity and cultivation are ſo little taken into the account, that writing a book ſeems to be now conſidered as the only ſure reſource which the idle and the illiterate have always in their power.

May the Author be indulged in a ſhort digreſſion while ſhe remarks, though rather out of its place, that the corruption occaſioned fioned by thefe books has fpread fo wide, and defcended fo low, as to have become one of the moft univerfal as well as moft pernicious fources of corruption among us. Not only among milleners, mantua-makers, and other trades where numbers work together, the labour of one girl is frequently facrificed that fhe may be fpared to read thofe mifchievous books to the others; but fhe has been affured by clergymen who have witneffed the fact, that they are procured and greedily read in the wards of our Hofpitals! an awful hint, that thofe who teach the poor to read, fhould not only take care to furnifh them with principles which will lead them to abhor corrupt books, but that they fhould alfo furnifh them with fuch books as fhall ftrengthen and confirm their principles*. And let every

* The above facts furnifh no argument on the fide of thofe who would keep the poor in ignorance. Thofe who cannot *read* can *hear*, and are likely to hear to worfe purpofe than thofe who have been better taught. And that ignorance furnifhes no fecurity

every Chriftian remember, that there is no
other way of entering truly into the fpirit of
that divine prayer, which petitions that the
name of God may be " hallowed," that
" his kingdom (of grace) may come," and
that " his will may be done on earth as it
" is in heaven," than by each individual
contributing accoiding to his meafure to
accomplifh the work for which he prays;
for to pray that thefe great objects may be
promoted, without contributing to their
promotion by our exertions, our money,
and our influence, is a palpable inconfiftency.

---

fecurity for integrity either in morals or politics,
the late revolts in more than one country, remarkable
for the ignorance of the poor, fully illuftrate. It is
earneftly hoped that the above facts may tend to imprefs ladies with the importance of fuperintending
the inftruction of the poor, and of making it an indifpenfable part of their chaiity to give them moral and
religious books.

CHAP. VIII.

On the religious and moral use of history and geography.

BUT while every fort of ufeful knowledge fhould be carefully imparted to
young perfons, it fhould be imparted not
merely for its own fake, but alfo for
the fake of its fubferviency to higher
things. All human learning fhould be
taught, not as an end, but a means; and
in this view even a leffon of hiftory or
geography may be converted into a leffon
of religion. In the ftudy of hiftory, the
inftructor will accuftom the pupil not
merely to ftore her memory with facts and
anecdotes, and to afcertain dates and
epochas; but fhe will accuftom her alfo to
trace effects to their caufes, to examine the
fecret fprings of action, and accurately to

VOL. I. o obferve

obferve the operation of the paffions. It is only meant to notice here fome few of the moral benefits which may be derived from a judicious perufal of hiftory; and from among other points of inftruction, I felect the following:

The ftudy of hiftory may ferve to give a clearer infight into the corruption of human nature:

It may fhow the *plan* of Providence in the direction of events, and in the ufe of unworthy inftruments:

It may affift in the *vindication* of Providence, in the common failure of virtue and the fuccefs of vice:

It may lead to a diftruft of our own judgment:

It may contribute to our improvement in felf-knowledge.

But to prove to the pupil the important doctrine of human corruption from the ftudy of hiftory, will require a truly Chriftian commentator; for, from the low ftandard of right eftablifhed by the gene-

rality

rality of hiftorians, who erect fo many
perfons into good characters who fall
fhort of the true idea of Chriftian virtue,
the unaffifted reader will be liable to
form very imperfect views of what is real
goodnefs; and will conclude, as his author
fometimes does, that the true idea of
human nature is to be taken from the
medium between his beft and his worft
characters; without acqiruing a juft notion
of that prevalence of evil, which, in fpite
of thofe few brighter luminaries that here
and there juft ferve to gild the gloom
of hiftory, tends abundantly to eftablifh
the doctrine. It will indeed be continually
eftablifhing itfelf by thofe who, in perufing
the hiftory of mankind, carefully mark the
rife and progrefs of fin, from the firft timid
irruption of an evil thought, to the fearlefs
accomplifhment of the abhorred crime in
which that thought has ended: from the
indignant queftion, " Is thy fervant a dog
" that he fhould do this great thing * ?"

* 2 Kings, viii. 13.

to the perpetration of that very enormity of which he could not endure the flighteſt ſuggeſtion.

In this connection may it not be obſerved, that young perſons ſhould be put on their guard againſt a too implicit belief in the flattering accounts which ſome voyage-writers are fond of exhibiting of the virtue, amiableneſs, and benignity of ſome of the countries newly diſcovered by our circumnavigators, the ſuperior goodneſs aſcribed to the Hindoos, and particularly the account of the inhabitants of the Pellew Iſlands? Theſe laſt indeed have been almoſt repreſented as having eſcaped the univerſal taint of our common nature, and would ſeem by their purity to have ſprung from another anceſtor than Adam.

One cannot forbear ſuſpecting that theſe pleaſing but ſomewhat overcharged portraits of man, in his natural ſtate, are drawn with the invidious deſign, by counteracting the doctrine of human corruption,

corruption, to degrade the value and even deftroy the neceffity of the Chriftian religion. That in countries profeffing Chriftianity, very many are not Chriftians will be too readily granted. Yet, to fay nothing of the vaft fuperiority of goodnefs in the lives of thofe who are really governed by Chriftianity, is there not fomething even in her reflex light which guides to greater purity many of thofe who do not profefs to walk by it? I doubt much, if numbers of the unbelievers of a Chriftian country, from the founder views and better h bits derived incidentally and collaterally as it were, from the influence of a Gofpel, the truth of which however they do not acknoweledge, would not ftart at many of the actions which thefe *heathen perfectionifts* daily commit without hefitation.

The religious reader of general hiftory will obferve the controlling hand of Providence in the direction of events, and in turning the moft unworthy actions and

inftru-

inftruments to the accomplifhment of his own purpofes. She will mark infinite Wifdom directing what appears to be cafual occurrences, to the completion of his own plan. She will point out how caufes feemingly the moft unconnected, events feemingly the moft unpromifing, circum-ftances feemingly the moft incongruous, are all working together for fome final good. She will mark how national as well as individual crimes are often over-ruled to fome hidden purpofe far different from the intention of the actors: how Omnipotence can and often does bring about the beft purpofes by the worft in-ftruments: how the bloody and unjuft conqueror is but " the rod of His wrath," to punifh or to purify his offending chil-dren: how " the fury of the oppreffor," and the fufferings of the oppreffed, will one day vindicate His righteous dealings. She will unfold to the lefs enlightened reader, how infinite Wifdom often mocks the infignificance of human greatnefs, and the

fhallow

shallowness of human ability, by setting
aside instruments the most powerful, while
He works by agents comparatively con-
temptible. But she will carefully guard
this doctrine of Divine Providence, thus
working out his own purposes through the
sins of his creatures, and by the instru-
mentality of the wicked, by calling to
mind, while the offender is but a tool in
the hands of the great Artificer, " the woe
" denounced against him by whom the of-
" fence cometh!" She will explain how
those mutations and revolutions in states
which appear to us so unaccountable, and
how those operations of Providence which
seem to us so entangled and complicated,
all move harmoniously and in perfect order:
that there is not an event but has its
commission; not a misfortune which
breaks its allotted rank ; not a trial which
moves out of its appointed track. While
calamities and crimes seem to fly in casual
confusion, all is commanded or permitted ;
all is under the control of a wisdom which

cannot

cannot err, of a goodnefs which cannot do
wrong

To explain my meaning by a few inftances. When the fpirit of the youthful
reader rifes in honeft indignation at that
hypocritical piety which divorced an un-
offending Queen to make way for the
lawfu! crime of our eighth Henry's marriage with Ann Boleyn; and when that
indignation is increafed by the more open
profligacy which brought about the execution of the latter; the inftructor will not
lofe fo fair an occafion for unfolding how
in the councils of the Moft High the
crimes of the King were overruled to the
happinefs of the country; and how, to
this inaufpicious marriage, from which the
heroic Elizabeth fprung, the Proteftant
religion owed its firm ftability.

She will explain to her, how even the
conquefts of ambition, after having deluged
a land with blood, and involved the perpe-
tra.or in guilt, and the innocent victim in
ruin, may yet be made the inftruments of
opening

opening to future generations the way to commerce, to civilization, to Chriftianity. She may remind her, as they are following Cæfar in his invafion of Britain, that whereas the conqueror fancied he was only gratifying his own inordinate ambition, extending the flight of the Roman Eagle, immortalizing his own name, and proving that " this world was made for Cæfar;" he was in reality becoming the effectual though unconfcious inftrument of leading a land of barbarians to civilization and to fcience: and was in fact preparing an ifland of Pagans to embrace the religion of Chrift. She will inform her, that when the above-named victorious nation had made Judea a Roman province, and the Jews had become their tributaries, the Romans did not know, nor did the indignant Jews fufpect, that this circumftance was operating to the confirmation of an event the moft important the world ever faw.

For when " Auguftus fent forth a decree " that all the world fhould be taxed;"

he

he vainly thought he was only enlarging his own imperial power, whereas he
was acting in unconfcious fubfervience to
the decree of a higher Sovereign, and was
helping to afcertain by a public act the
exact period of Chrift's birth, and furnifhing a record of his extraction from
that family from which it was predicted
by a long line of Prophets that he fhould
fpring. Herod's atrocious murder of
the innocents has added an additional
circumftance for the confirmation of
our faith; the incredulity of Thomas has
ftrengthened our belief; nay, the treachery
of Judas, and the injuftice of Pilate, were
the human inftruments employed for the
falvation of the world.

The youth that is not armed with
Chriftian principles, will be tempted to
mutiny not only againft the juftice, but the
very exiftence of a fuperintending Providence, in contemplating thofe frequent
inftances which occur in hiftory of the
ill fuccefs of the more virtuous caufe,
and

and the profperity of the wicked.   He will
fee with aftonifhment that it is Rome which
triumphs,   while   Carthage,   which   had
clearly   the   better   caufe,   falls.   Now and
then indeed a Cicero prevails, and a Cataline is fubdued : but often, it is Cæfar fuccefsful againft the fomewhat jufter preten-
fions of Pompey, and againft the ftill
clearer caufe of Cato.   It is Octavius who
triumphs,   and   it   is   over   Brutus   that   he
triumphs !   It is Tiberius that is enthroned,
while Germanicus falls !

Thus his faith in a righteous Providence
at firft view is ftaggered, and he is ready
to fay, " Surely it is not God that governs
" the earth!" But on a fuller confideration,
(and   here   the   fuggeftions   of   a   Chriftian
inftructor   are   peculiarly   wanted,)   there
will   appear   great   wifdom   in   this   very
confufion of vice and virtue; for it is
calculated to fend one's thoughts forward
to a world of retribution, the principle
of retribution being fo imperfectly eftablifhed in this.   It is indeed fo far common   for   virtue   to   have   the   advantage
here,

here, in point of happinefs at leaft, though not of glory, that the courfe of Providence is ftill calculated to prove that God is on the fide of virtue; but ftill, virtue is fo often unfuccefsful, that clearly the God of virtue, in order that his work may be perfect, muft have in referve a world of retribution. This confufed ftate of things therefore is juft that ftate which is moft of all calculated to confirm the deeply confiderate mind in the belief of a future ftate : for if all were even here, or very nearly fo, fhould we not fay, " Juftice is already fatisfied, " and there *needs* no other world ?" On the other hand, if vice always triumphed, fhould we not then be ready to argue in favour of vice rather than virtue, and to *wifh* for no other world ?

It feems, fo very important to ground young perfons in the belief that they will not inevitably meet in this world with reward and fuccefs according to their merit, but to habituate them to expect even the moft virtuous attempts to be often, though not always difappointed, that I am in danger of of tautology on this point. This fact is precisely what hiftory teaches. The truth fhould be plainly told to the young reader ; and the antidote to that evil, which miftaken and worldly people would expect to arife from divulging this difcouraging doctrine, is *faith*. The importance of faith there- fore, and the neceffity of it to real, unbend- ing, and perfevering virtue, is furely made plain by profane hiftory itfelf. For the fame thing which happens to ftates and kings, happens to private life and to indi- viduals. Thus there is fcarcely a page, even of Pagan Hiftory, which may not be made inftrumental to the eftablifhing of the truth of revelation : and it is only by fuch a mode of inftruction that fome of the evils of the ftudy of ancient literature can be obviated.

Diftruft and diffidence in our own judg- ment feems to be alfo an important in- ftruction to be learnt from hiftory. How contrary to all expectation do the events therein recorded commonly turn out ? and

yet

yet we proceed to foretel this and that event from the appearances of things under our own obfervation, with the fame arrogant certainty as if we had never been warned by the monitory annals of mankind.

There is fcarcely one great event in hiftory which does not, in the iffue, produce effects upon which human forefight could never have calculated. The fuccefs of Auguftus againft his country produced peace in many diftant provinces, who thus ceafed to be haraffed and tormented by this oppreffive republic. Could this effect have been forefeen, it might have fobered the defpair of Cato, and checked the vehemence of Brutus. In politics, in fhort in every thing except in morals and religion, all is, to a confiderable degree, uncertain. This reafoning is not meant to fhew that Cato ought not to have *fought*, but that he ought not to have *defponded* even after the laft battle; and certainly, even upon his own principles, ought not to have killed himfelf. It would be departing too much

from

from my object to apply this argument,
however obvious the application, againſt
thoſe who were driven to unreaſonable dif-
truſt and deſpair by the late ſucceſſes of a
neighbouring nation.

But all knowledge will be comparatively of little value, if we neglect ſelf-
knowledge; and of ſelf-knowledge hiſtory
and biography may be made ſucceſsful
vehicles. It will be to little purpoſe that
our pupils become accurate critics on the
characters of others, while they remain ignorant of themſelves; for while to thoſe
who exerciſe a habit of ſelf-application a
book of profane hiſtory may be made an
inſtrument of improvement in this difficult
ſcience; ſo without this habit the Bible
itſelf may, in this view, be read with little
profit.

It will be to no purpoſe that the reader
weeps over the fortitude of the Chriſtian
hero, or the conſtancy of the martyr, if
ſhe do not bear in mind that ſhe herſelf is
called to endure her own common trials
with

with fomething of the fame temper: if fhe do not bear in mind that, to control irregular humours, and to fubmit to the daily vexations of life, will require, though in a lower degree, the exertion of the fame principle, and fupplication for the aid of the fame fpirit which fuftained the Chriftian hero in the trying conflicts of life, or the martyr in his agony at the ftake.

May I be permitted to fuggeft a few in-ftances, by way of fpecimen, how both facred and common hiftory may tend to promote felf-knowledge? And let me again remind the warm admirer of fuffer-ing piety under extraordinary trials, that if fhe now fail in the petty occafions to which fhe is actually called out, fhe would not be likely to have ftood in thofe more trying occafions which excite her admi-ration.

While fhe is applauding the felf-deny-ing faint who renounced his eafe, or chofe to embrace death, rather than violate his duty, let her afk herfelf if fhe has never refufed

refufed to fubmit to the paltry inconve-
nience of giving up her company, or even
altering her dinner-hour on a Sunday,
though by this trifling facrifice her family
might have been enabled to attend the
public worſhip in the afternoon.

While ſhe reads with horror that Bel-
ſhazzar was rioting with his thouſand no-
bles at the very moment when the Perſian
army was burſting through the brazen
gates of Babylon ; is ſhe very fure that ſhe
herfelf, in an almoſt equally imminent
moment of public danger, has not been
nightly indulging in every fpecies of diſſi-
pation ?

When ſhe is deploring the inconſiſtency
of the human heart, while ſhe contraſts
Mark Anthony's bravery and contempt of
eafe at one period, with his licentious indulgences at another ; or while ſhe la-
ments over the intrepid foul of Cæfar,
whom ſhe had been following in his painful marches, or admiring in his contempt
of death, diſſolved in diſſolute pleafures

VOL. I.   P   with

with the enfnaring Queen of Egypt; let
her examine whether fhe herfelf has never,
though in a much lower degree, evinced
fomething of the fame inconfiftency? whether fhe who lives perhaps an orderly,
fober, and reafonable life during her fum-
mer refidence in the country, does not
plunge with little fcruple in the winter into
all the moft extravagant pleafures of the
capital? whether fhe never carries about
with her an accommodating kind of religion, which can be made to bend to places
and feafons, to climates and cuftoms;
which takes its tinÐure from the fafhion
without, and not its habits from the principle within; which is decent with the
pious, fober with the orderly, and loofe
with the licentious?

While fhe is admiring the generofity of
Alexander in giving away kingdoms and
provinces, let her, in order to afcertain
whether fhe could imitate this magnani-
mity, take heed if fhe herfelf is daily feizing all the little occafions of doing good,
which

which every day prefents to the affluent?
Her call is not to facrifice a province;
but does fhe facrifice an opera ticket?
She who is not doing all the good fhe
can under her prefent circumftances, would
not do all fhe forefees fhe could, in ima-
ginary ones, were her power enlarged to
the extent of her wifhes.

While fhe is inveighing with patriotic
indignation, that in a neighbouring metropolis thirty theatres were open every night
in time of war and public calamity, is fhe
very clear, that in a metropolis which
contains only three, fhe was not almoft
conftantly at one of them in time of war
and public calamity alfo? For though in
a national view it may make a wide difference whether there be in the capital three
theatres or thirty, yet, as the fame perfon
can only go to one of them at once, it
makes but little difference as to the quan-
tum of diffipation in the individual. She
who rejoices at fuccefsful virtue in a hiftory, or at the profperity of a perfon

whole

whofe interefts do not interfere with her own, may exercife her felf-knowledge, by examining whether fhe rejoices equally at the happinefs of every one about her; and let her remember fhe does not rejoice at it in the true fenfe, if fhe does not labour to promote it. She who glows with rapture at a virtuous charaĉter in hiftory, fhould afk her own heart, whether fhe is equally ready to do juftice to the fine qualities of her acquaintance, though fhe may not particularly love them; and whether fhe takes unfeigned pleafure in the fuperior talents, virtues, fame, and fortune of thofe whom fhe profeffes to love, though fhe is eclipfed by them?

*　*　*　*　*　*　*

In like manner, in the ftudy of geography and natural hiftory, the attention fhould be habitually turned to the goodnefs of Providence, who commonly adapts the various produĉtions of climates to the peculiar

peculiar wants of the refpective inhabitants.
To illuftrate my meaning by one or two
inftances out of a thoufand. The reader
may be led to admire the confiderate goodnefs of Providence in having caufed the
fpiry fir, whofe flender foliage does not
obftruct the beams of the fun, to grow in
the dreary regions of the North, whofe
fhivering inhabitants could fpare none of
its fcanty rays; while in the torrid zone,
the palm-tree, the plantane, and the
banana, fpread their umbrella leaves to
break the almoft intolerable fervors of a
vertical fun. How the camel, who is the
fole carrier of all the merchandife of
Turkey, Perfia, Egypt, Arabia, and Bar-
bary, who is obliged to tranfport his incredible burthens through countries in
which pafture is fo rare, can fubfift twenty-
four hours without food, and can travel,
loaded, many days without water, through
dry and dufty deferts, which fupply none;
and all this, not from the habit but from
the conformation of the animal : for Na-

turalifts make this conformity of powers
to climates a rule of judgment in afcertaining the native countries of animals,
and always determine it to be that to which
their powers and properties are moft appropriate.

Thus the writers of natural hiftory are
perhaps unintentionally magnifying the
operations of Providence, when they infift
that animals do not modify and give way
to the influence of other climates; but
here they too commonly ftop; negleƈting,
or perhaps refufing, to afcribe to infinite
goodnefs this wife and merciful accommodation; and here the pious inftruƈtor will
come in, in aid of their deficiency: for
Philofophers too feldom trace up caufes,
and wonders, and bleffings to their Author.
And it is peculiarly to be regretted that a
late juftly celebrated French Naturalift,
who, though not famous for his accuracy,
poffeffed fuch diverfified powers of defcription that he had the talent of making
the drieft fubjeƈts interefting; together
with

with fuch a livelinefs of delineation, that
his characters of animals are drawn with a
fpirit and variety rather to be looked for
in an hiftorian of men than of beafts : it is
to be regretted that this w.iter, with all
his excellencies, is abfolutely inadmiffible
into the library of a young lady, both on
account of his immodefty and his impiety ;
and if, in wifhing to exclude him, it may
be thought wrong to have given him fo
much commendation, it is only meant to
fhow that the author is not led to repro-
bate his principles from infenfibility to his
talents. The remark is rather made to
put the reader on remembering that no
brilliancy of genius, no diverfity of attainments, fhould ever be allowed as a commutation for defective principles and corrupt ideas *.

---

* Goldfmith's Hiftory of animated Nature has
many references to a Divine Author. It is to be
wifhed that fome judicious perfon would publifh a
new edition of this work, purified from the indelicate
and offenfive parts.

CHAP. IX.

*On the use of definitions, and the moral
benefits of accuracy in language.*

" Persons having been accuftomed from
" their cradles to learn words before they
" knew the ideas for which they ftand,
" ufually continue to do fo all their lives,
" never taking the pains to fettle in their
" minds the determined ideas which be-
" long to them. This want of a precife
" fignification in their words, when they
" come to reafon, *efpecially in moral*
" *matters,* is the caufe of very obfcure and
" uncertain notions. They ufe thefe un-
" determined words confidently, without
" much troubling their heads about a
" certain fixed meaning, whereby, befides
" the eafe of it, they obtain this advantage,
" that as in fuch difcourfe they are feldom
" in

" in the right, fo they are as feldom to be
" convinced that they are in the wrong, it
" being juft the fame to go about to draw
" thofe perfons out of their miftakes, who
" have no fettled notions, as to difpoffefs
" a vagrant of his habitation who has no
" fettled abode.——The chief end of lan-
" guage being to be underftood, words
" ferve not for that end when they do not
" excite in the hearer the fame idea which
" they ftand for in the mind of the
" fpeaker *."

I have chofen to fhelter myfelf under
the broad fanction of the great Author here
quoted, with a view to apply this rule
in philology to a moral purpofe; for
it applies to the veracity of converfation as
much as to its correctnefs ; and as ftrongly
recommends unequivocal and fimple truth,
as accurate and juft expreffion. Scarcely
any one perhaps has an adequate conception how much clear and correct ex-

* Locke.

preffions

preſſions favour the elucidation of truth;
and the ſide of truth is obviouſly the ſide
of morals; it is in façt one and the ſame
cauſe; and it is of courſe the ſame cauſe
with that of true religion alſo.

It is therefore no worthleſs part of education to ſtudy the preciſe meaning of
words, and the appropriate ſignification of
language. To this end I know no better
method than to accuſtom young perſons
very early to a habit of defining common
words and things; for, as definition ſeems
to lie at the root of correctneſs, to be accuſtomed to define Engliſh words in Engliſh, would improve the underſtanding
more than barely to know what thoſe words
are called in French or Italian. Or rather,
one uſe of learning other languages is,
becauſe definition is often involved in
etymology; that is, ſince many Engliſh
words take their derivation from foreign
languages, they cannot be ſo accurately
underſtood without ſome knowledge of
thoſe languages: but preciſion of any
kind,

kind, either moral or philological, too seldom finds its way into the education of women.

It is perhaps going out of my province to obferve, that it might be well if young *men* alfo, before they entered on the world, were to be furnifhed with correct definitions of certain words, the ufe of which is become rather ambiguous. For inftance; they fhould be provided with a good definition of the word *honour* in the fafhionable fenfe, fhewing what vices it includes, and what virtues it does not include: the term *good company*, which even the courtly Petronius of our days has defined as fometimes including not a few immoral and difreputable characters; *religion*, which in the various fenfes affigned it by the world, fometimes means fuperftition, fometimes fanaticifm, and fometimes a mere difpofition to attend on any kind of form of worfhip: the word *goodnefs*, which is made to mean every thing that is not notorioufly bad; and fometimes even that

too,

too, if what is notorioully bad be accom-
panied by good humour, pleafing manners, and a little alms-giving. By thefe
means they would go forth armed againft
many of the falfe opinions which through
the abufe or ambiguous meaning of words
pafs fo current in the world.

But to return to the youthful part of
that fex which is the more immediate
object of this little work. With correct
definition they fhould alfo be taught to
ftudy the fhades of words, and this not
merely with a view to accuracy of expreffion, but to moral truth.

It may be thought ridiculous to affert,
that morals have any connection with the
purity of language, or that the precifion of
truth may be violated through defect of
critical exactnefs in the three degrees of
comparifon : yet how frequently do we
hear from the dealers in fuperlatives, of
" moft admirable, fuper-excellent, and
" quite perfect" people, who, to plain
perfons, not bred in the fchool of ex-
aggeration,

aggeration, would appear mere common
characters, not rising above the level
of mediocrity! By this negligence in the
juft application of words, we fhall be
as much mifled by thefe trope and figure
ladies, when they degrade as when they
panegyrize ; for to a plain and fober.
judgment, a tradefman may not be " the
" moft good-for-nothing fellow that ever
" exifted," merely becaufe it was impoffible for him to execute in an hour an order
which required a week ; a lady may not be
" the moft hideous fright the world ever
" faw," though the make of her gown
may have been obfolete for a month ; nor
may one's young friend's father be " a
" monfter of cruelty," though he may be
a quiet gentleman who does not choofe to
live at watering-places, but likes to have
his daughter ftay at home with him in the
country.

But of all the parts of fpeech the inter-
jection is the moft abundantly in ufe with
the hyperbolical fair ones. Would it
                                    could

could be added that thefe emphatical expletives (if I may make ufe of a contradictory term) were not fometimes tinctured with profanenefs! Though I am perfuaded that idle habit is more at the bottom of this deep offence than intended impiety, yet there is fcarcely any error of youthful talk which wants feverer caftigation. And an habit of exclamation fhould be rejected by polifhed people as vulgar, even if it were not abhorred as profane.

The habit of exaggerating trifles, together with the grand female failing of exceffive mutual flattery, and elaborate general profeffions of fondnefs and attachment, is inconceivably cherifhed by the voluminous private correfpondences in which fome girls are indulged. A facility of ftyle, and an eafy turn of expreffion, are acquifitions faid to be derived from an early interchange of fentiments by letter-writing; but thefe would be dearly purchafed by the facrifice of that truth, fobriety, and correctnefs of language, and

2   that

that ingenuous fimplicity of character and manners fo lovely in female youth.

But antecedent to this *epiftolary period* of life, they fhould have been accuftomed to the moft fcrupulous exactnefs in whatever they relate. They fhould maintain the moft critical accuracy in *facts*, in *dates*, in *numbering*, in *defcribing*, in fhort, in whatever pertains, either directly or indirectly, clofely or remotely, to the great fundamental principle, *Truth*. It is fo very difficult for perfons of great livelinefs to reftrain themfelves within the fober limits of ftrict veracity, either in their affertions or narrations, efpecially when a little undue indulgence of fancy is apt to procure for them the praife of genius and fpirit, that this reftraint is one of the earlieft principles which fhould be worked into the youthful mind.

The converfation of young females is alfo in danger of being overloaded with epithets. As in the warm feafon of youth hardly any thing is feen in the true point of vifion,

vifion, fo hardly any thing is named in naked fimplicity; and the very fenfibility of the feelings is partly a caufe of the extravagance of the expreffion. But here, as in other points, the facred writers, particularly of the New Teftament, prefent us with the pureft models; and its natural and unlaboured ftyle of expreffion is perhaps not the meaneft evidence of the truth of the Gofpel. There is throughout the whole narratives, no overcharged character, no elaborate defcription, nothing ftudicufly emphatical, as if truth of itfelf were weak, and wanted to be helped out. There is little panegyric, and lefs invective; none but on great, and awful, and juftifiable occafions. The authors record their own faults with the fame honefty as if they were the faults of other men, and the faults of other men with as little amplification as if they were their own. There is perhaps no book in which adjectives are fo fparingly ufed. A modeft ftatement of the fact, with no colouring and little comment,

ment, with little emphafis and no varnifh, is the example held out to us for correcting the exuberances of paffion and of language, by that divine volume which furnifhes us with the ftill more important rule of faith and ftandard of practice. Nor is the truth lowered by any feeblenefs, nor the fpirit diluted, nor the impreffion weakened by this fobernefs and moderation; for with all this plainnefs there is fo much force, that a few fimple touches and artlefs ftrokes of Scripture characters convey a ftronger outline of the perfon delineated, than is fometimes given by the moft elaborate and finifhed portrait of more artificial hiftorians.

If it be objected to this remark, that many parts of the facred writings abound in a lofty, figurative, and even hyperbolical ftyle; this objection applies chiefly to the writings of the Old Teftament, and to the prophetical and poetical parts of that. But the metaphorical and florid ftyle of thofe writings is diftinct from the inaccurate and over-ftrained expreffion we have

been cenfuring ; for that only is inaccu-
racy which leads to a falfe and inadequate
conception in the reader or hearer. The
lofty ftyle of the Eaftern, and of other heroic poetry, does not fo miflead ; for the
metaphor is underftood to be a metaphor,
and the imagery is underftood to be ornamental. The ftyle of the Scriptures of the
Old Teftament is not, it is true, plain in
oppofition to figurative, nor fimple in oppofition to florid; but it is plain and fimple
in the beft fenfe, as oppofed to falfe principles and falfe tafte ; it raifes no wrong
idea ; it gives an exact impreffion of the
thing it means to convey ; and its very
tropes and figures, though bold, are never
unnatural or affected : when it embellifhes
it does not miflead ; even when it exag-
gerates, it does not mifreprefent ; if it be
hyperbolical, it is fo either in compliance
with the genius of Oriental language, or in
compliance with contemporary cuftoms, or
becaufe the fubject is one which will be
moft forcibly impreffed by a ftrong figure.
The loftinefs of the expreffion deducts nothing

thing from the weight of the circumftance; the imagery animates the reader without mifleading him; the boldeft illuftration, while it dilates his conception of the fubject, detracts nothing from its fimplicity; and truth, inftead of being injured by the opulence of the figures, contrives to make them frefh and varied avenues to the heart and the underftanding.

CHAP. X.

On Religion.—The neceſſity and duty of early inſtruction ſhewn by analogy with human learning.

I T has been the faſhion of our late inno-vators in philoſophy, who have written ſome of the moſt brilliant and popular treatiſes on education, to decry the prac-tice of early inſtilling religious knowledge into the minds of children : it has been alledged that it is of the utmoſt importance to the cauſe of truth, that the mind of man ſhould be kept free from prepoſſeſſions ; and in particular, that every one ſhould be left to form ſuch judgment on religious ſubjects as may ſeem beſt to his own reaſon in maturer years.

This ſentiment has received ſome coun-tenance from thoſe better characters who
have

have wifhed, on the faireft principle, to encourage free inquiry in religion ; but it has been pufhed to the blameable excefs here cenfured, chiefly by the new philofophers ; who, while they profefs only an ingenuous zeal for truth, are in fact flily endeavouring to deftroy Chriftianity itfelf, by difcountenancing, under the plaufible pretence of free inquiry, all attention whatever to the religious education of our youth.

It is undoubtedly our duty, while we are inftilling principles into the tender mind, to take peculiar care that thofe principles be found and juft ; that the religion we teach be the religion of the Bible, and not the inventions of human error or fuperftition : that the principles we infufe into others, be fuch as we ourfelves have well fcrutinized, and not the refult of our credulity or bigotry ; nor the mere hereditary, unexamined prejudices of our own undifcerning childhood. It may alfo be granted, that it is the duty of every parent to inform the youth, that when his facul-

ties

ties shall have so unfolded themselves, as to enable him to examine for himself those principles which the parent is now instilling, it will be his duty so to examine them.

But after making these concessions, I would most seriously insist that there are certain leading and fundamental truths; that there are certain sentiments on the side of Christianity, as well as of virtue and benevolence, in favour of which every child *ought* to be prepossessed; and may it not be also added, that to expect to keep the mind void of all prepossession, even upon any subject, appears to be altogether a vain and impracticable attempt ? an attempt, the very suggestion of which argues much ignorance of human nature.

Let it be observed here, that we are not combating the infidel; that we are not producing evidences and arguments in *favour* of Christianity, or trying to win over the assent of the reader to that which he disputes; but that we are taking it for

granted,

granted, not only that Chriftianity is true, but that we are addreffing thofe who believe it to be true : an affumption which has been made throughout this work. Affuming, therefore, that there are religious principles which are true, and which ought to be communicated in the moft effectual manner, the next queftion which arifes feems to be, at what age and in what manner thefe ought to be inculcated ? That it ought to be at an early period we have both the example and the command of Chrift; for he himfelf attended his parents in their annual public devotions at Jerufalem during his own infancy; and afterwards in his public miniftration encouragingly faid, " Suffer *little* children to come unto me."

But here conceding for the fake of argument what yet cannot be conceded, that fome good reafons *may* be brought in favour of delay; allowing that fuch impreffions as are communicated early may not be very deep; allowing them even to become totally effaced by the fubfequent

corrup-

corruptions of the heart and of the world;
still I would illustrate the importance of
early infusing religious knowledge, by an
allusion drawn from the power of early
habit in human learning. Put the case,
for instance, of a person who was betimes
initiated in the rudiments of classical studies.
Suppose him after quitting school to have
fallen, either by a course of idleness or of
vulgar pursuits, into a total neglect of
study. Should this person at any future
period happen to be called to some profession, which should oblige him, as we
say, to rub up his Greek and Latin; his
memory still retaining the unobliterated
though faint traces of his early pursuits, he
will be able to recover his neglected learning with less difficulty than he could now
begin to learn; for he is not again obliged
to set out with studying the simple elements; they come back on being pursued; they are found on being searched
for; the decayed images assume shape, and
strength, and colour; he has in his mind
firstt

firſt principles to which to recur; the rules of grammar which he has allowed himſelf to violate, he has not however forgotten; he will recall neglected ideas, he will reſume ſlighted habits far more eaſily than he could now begin to acquire new ones. I appeal to Clergymen who are called to attend the dying beds of ſuch as have been bred in groſs and ſtupid ignorance of religion, for the juſtneſs of this compariſon. Do they not find that theſe unhappy people have no ideas in common with them? that *they* poſſeſs no intelligible medium by which to make themſelves underſtood? that the perſons to whom they are addreſſing themſelves have no firſt principles to which they can be referred? that they are ignorant not only of the ſcience, but the language of Chriſtianity?

But at worſt, whatever be the event to the child, though in general we are encouraged, from the tenor of Scripture and the courſe of experience, to hope that

that

that event would be favourable, is it nothing for the parent to have acquitted himfelf of this prime duty? And will not the
parent who fo acquits himfelf, with better
reafon and more lively hope, fupplicate the
Father of mercies for the reclaiming of a
prodigal, who has wandered out of that
right path in which he has fet him forward,
than for the converfion of a neglected
creature, to whofe feet the Gofpel had
never been offered as a light? And how
different will be the dying reflections even
of that parent whofe earneft endeavours
have been unhappily defeated by the fubfequent and voluntary perverfion of his
child, from his who will reafonably aggra-
vate his pangs by transferring the fins of his
neglected child to the number of his own
tranfgreffions.

And to fuch well-intentioned but ill-
judging parents as really wifh their children to be hereafter pious, but erroneoufly
withhold inftruction till the more advanced
period prefcribed by the great mafter of

fplendid

fplendid paradoxes * fhall arrive ; who can
affure them that while they are withholding
the good feed, the great and ever vigilant
enemy, who affiduoufly feizes hold on every
opportunity which *we* flight, and cultivates
every advantage which *we* negleft, may not
be ftocking the fallow ground with tares ?
Nay, who in this fluftuating fcene of things
can be affured, even if this were not certainly to be the cafe, that to them the promifed period ever fhall arrive at all ? Who
fhall afcertain to them that their now ne-
glefted child fhall certainly live to receive
the delayed inftruftion ? Who can affure
them that they themfelves will live to communicate it ?

It is almoft needlefs to obferve that
parents who are indifferent about religion,
much more thofe who treat it with fcorn,
are not likely to be anxious on this fub-
jeft ; it is therefore the attention of *religious* parents which is here chiefly called

* Rouffeau.

upon ;

upon; and the more fo, as there feems, on this point, an unaccountable negligence in many of thefe, whether it arife from indolence, falfe principles, or whatever other motive.

But independent of knowledge, it is fomething, nay, let philofophers fay what they will, it is much, to give youth *prepoffeffions* in favour of religion, to fecure their *prejudices* on its fide befo e you turn them adrift into the world; a world in which, before they can be completely armed with arguments and reafons, they will be affailed by numbers whofe prepoffeffions and prejudices, far more than *their* arguments and reafons, attach them to the other fide. Why fhould not the Chriftian youth furnifh himfelf in a good caufe with the fame natural armour which the enemies of religion wear in a bad one? It is certain that to fet out with fentiments in favour of the religion of our country is no more an error or a weaknefs, than to grow up with a fondnefs for our country itfelf.

If

If the love of our country be judged a fair principle, furely a Chriftian, who is " a citizen of no mean city," may lawfully have *his* attachments too. If patriotifm be an honeft prejudice, Chriftianity is not a fervile one. Nay, let us teach the youth to hug his prejudices rather than to acquire that verfatile and accommodating citizenfhip of the world, by which he may be an Infidel in Paris, a Papift at Rome, and a Muffulman at Cairo.

Let me not be fuppofed fo to elevate politics, or fo to deprefs religion, as to make any comparifon of the value of the one with the other, when I obferve, that between the true Britifh patriot and the true Chriftian, there will be this common refemblance : the more deeply each of them inquires, the more will he be confirmed in his refpective attachment, the one to his country, the other to his religion. I fpeak with reverence of the immeafurable diftance ; but the more the one preffes on the firm arch of our conftitution,

and

and the other on that of Chriftianity, the
ftronger he will find them both. Each
challenges fcrutiny; each has nothing
to dread but from fhallow politicians, and
fhallow philofophers; in each intimate
knowledge juftifies prepoffeffion; in each
inveftigation confirms attachment.

If we divide the human being into three
component parts, the bodily, the intellectual, and the fpiritual, is it not reafonable
that a portion of care and attention be
affigned to each in fome degree adequate
to its importance? Should I venture to
fay a *due* portion, a portion adapted to the
real comparative value of each, would not
that condemn in one word the whole
fyftem of modern education? Yet the rational and intellectual part being avowedly
more valuable than the bodily, while the
fpiritual and immortal part exceeds even
the intellectual ftill more than that fur-
paffes what is corporeal; is it then acting
according to the common rules of proportion; is it acting on the principles of
diftri-

diſtributive juſtice; is it acting with that
good fenfe and right judgment with which
the ordinary bufinefs of this world is
uſually tranſacted, to give the larger proportion of time and care to that which
is worth the leaſt? Is it fair that what
relates to the body and the organs of
the body, I mean thoſe accompliſhments
which addreſs themſelves to the eye and the
ear, ſhould occupy almoſt the whole
thoughts; that the intellectual part ſhould
be robbed of its due proportion, and that
the ſpiritual part ſhould have almoſt no
proportion at all? Is not this preparing
your children for an awful diſappointment
in the tremendous day when they ſhall be
ſtripped of that body, of thoſe fenſes and
organs, which have been made almoſt the
ſole objects of their attention, and ſhall feel
themſelves left in poſſeſſion of nothing but
that ſpiritual part which in education was
ſcarcely taken into the account of their
exiſtence?

Surely

Surely it fhould be thought a reafonable compromife (and I am in fact under-valuing the object for the importance of which I plead) to fuggeft, that at leaft two thirds of that time which is now ufurped by externals, fhould be reftored to the rightful owners, the underftanding and the heart; and that the acquifition of religious knowledge in early youth, fhould at leaft be *no lefs* an object of fedulous attention than the cultivation of human learning or of outward embellifhments. It is alfo not unreafonable to fuggeft, that we fhould in Chriftianity, as in arts, fciences, or languages, begin with the beginning, fet out with the fimple elements, and thus " go on unto perfection."

Why in teaching to draw do you begin with ftrait lines and curves, till by gentle fteps the knowledge of outline and propor-tion be attained, and your picture be com-pleted; never lofing fight, however, of the elementary lines and curves? why in mufic do you fet out with the fimple notes, and

purfue

purſue the accuiſition through all its progreſs, ſtill in every ſtage recurring to the
notes? why in the ſcience of numbers do
you invent the ſimpleſt methods of convey-
ing juſt ideas of computation, ſtill referring
to the tables which involve the fundamental rules? why in the ſcience of
quantity do men introduce the pupil at firſt
to the plaineſt diagrams, and clear up one
difficulty before they allow another to
appear? why in teaching languages to
the youth do you ſeduiouſly infuſe into
his mind the rudiments of ſyntax? why
in parſing is he led to refer every word to
its part of ſpeech, to reſolve every ſentence
into its elements, to reduce every term to
its original, and from the firſt caſe of
nouns, and the firſt tenſe of verbs, to
explain their formations, changes, and de-
pendencies, till the principles of language
become ſo grounded, that, by continually
recurring to the rules, the ſpeaking and
writing correctly are fixed into a habit?
why all this, but becauſe you uniformly

wiſh

wifh him to be. grounded in each of his
acquirements? why, but becaufe you
are perfuaded that a flight, and flovenly,
and fuperficial, and irregular way of inftruction will never train him to excellence
in any thing?

Do young perfons then become mu-
ficians, and painters, and linguifts, and
mathematicians, by early ftudy and regular
labour; and fhall they become Chriftians
by accident? or rather, is not this acting
on that very principle of Dogberry, at
which you probably have often laughed?
Is not fuppofing that religion, like
" reading and writing, comes by Nature?"
Shall all thofe accomplifhments " which
" perifh in the ufing," be fo affiduoufly,
fo fyftematically taught? Shall all thefe
habits, which are limited to the things of
this world, be fo carefully formed, fo perfifted in, as to be interwoven with our very
make, fo as to become as it were a part of
ourfelves; and fhall that knowledge which
is to make us " wife unto falvation" be
picked

picked up at random, curforily, or perhaps
not picked up at all ? Shall that difficult
divine fcience which requires " line upon
" line, and precept upon precept," here
a little and there a little; that knowledge
which parents, even under a darker difpenfation, were required " to teach their chil-
" dren *diligently*, and to talk of it when
" they fat down in their houfe, and when
" they walked by the way, and when they
" lay down, and when they rofe up;'
fhall this knowledge be by Chriftian parents
deferred, or taught flightly ; or be fuperfeded by things of little comparative
worth ?

Shall the lively period of youth, the
foft and impreffible feafon when lafting
habits are formed, when the feal cuts
deep into the yielding wax, and the impreffion is more likely to be clear, and
ftrong, and lafting ; fhall this warm and
favourable feafon be fuffered to flide by,
without being turned to the great purpofe
for which not only youth, but life, and

breath,

breath, and being were beftowed? Shall
not that " faith without which it is impof-
" fible to pleafe God;" fhall not that
" holinefs without which no man can fee
" the Lord;" fhall not that knowledge
which is the foundation of faith and practice; fhall not that charity without which
all knowledge is founding brafs and a
tinkling cymbal, be impreffed, be inculcated, be enforced, as early, as conftantly,
as fundamentally, with the fame earneft
pufhing on to continual progrefs, with the
fame conftant reference to firft principles,
as are ufed in the cafe of thofe arts which
merely adorn human life? Shall we not
feize the happy period when the memory
is ftrong, the mind and all its powers vigorous and active, the imagination bufy and
all alive, the heart flexible, the temper
ductile, the confcience tender, curiofity
awake, fear powerful, hope eager, love
ardent; fhall we not feize this period for
inculcating that knowledge, and impreffing
thofe principles which are to form the
character,

character, and fix the deftination for eternity?

Or, if I may be allowed to addrefs another and a ftill more dilatory clafs, who are for procraftinating all concern about religion till we are driven to it by actual diftrefs, and who do not think of praying till they are perifhing, like the failor who faid, "he thought it was always "time enough to begin to pray when the "ftorm began." Of thefe I would afk, fhall we, with an unaccountable deliberation, defer our anxiety about religion till the bufy man or the diffipated woman are become fo immerfed in the cares of life, or fo entangled in its pleafures, that they will have little heart or fpirit to embrace a new principle? a principle whofe precife object it will be to condemn that very life into which they have already embarked; nay, to condemn almoft all that they have been doing and thinking ever fince they firft began to act or think? Shall we, I fay, begin now? or fhall we fuffer thofe

inftruc-

inftructions, to receive which requires all
the concentrated powers of a ftrong and
healthy mind, to be put off till the day of
excruciating pain, till the period of de-
bility and ftupefaction? Shall we wait
for that feafon, as if it were the moft
favourable for religious acquifitions, when
the fenfes fhall have been palled by
exceffive gratification, when the eye fhall
be tired with feeing, and the ear with
hearing? Shall we, when the whole man
is breaking up by difeafe or decay, expect
that the dim apprehenfion will difcern a
new fcience, or the obtufe feelings delight
themfelves with a new pleafure? a pleafure
too, not only incompatible with many of
the hitherto indulged pleafures, but one
which carries with it a ftrong intimation
that thofe pleafures terminate in the death
of the foul.

But, not to lofe fight of the important
analogy on which we have already dwelt fo
much; how prepofterous would it feem to
you to hear any one propofe to an illiterate
dying

dying man, to fet about learning even the
plaineft and eafieft rudiments of any new
art; to ftudy the mufical notes; to con-
jugate an auxiliary verb; to learn, not
the firft problem in Euclid, but even the
numeration table; and yet you do not
think it abfurd to poftpone religious inftruction, on principles which, if admitted
at all, muft terminate either in ignorance,
or in your propofing too late to a dying
man to begin to learn the totally unknown
fcheme of Chriftianity. You do not
think it impoffible that he fhould be
brought to liften to the " voice of this
" charmer," when he can no longer
liften to " the voice of finging men and
" finging women." You do not think
it unreafonable that immortal beings fhould
delay to devout their days to Heaven, till
they have " no pleafure in them" themfelves. You will not bring them to offer
up the firft fruits of their lips, and hearts,
and lives, to their Maker, becaufe you per-
fuade yourfelves that he who has called

himfelf

himfelf a " jealous God," may however
be contented hereafter with the wretched
facrifice of decayed appetites, and the
worthlefs leavings of almoft extinguifhed
affe&ions.

For one cannot believe, even with all
the melancholy procraftination we fee
around us, that there is fcarcely any one,
except he be a decided infidel, who does
not confider religion as at leaft a good re-
verfionary thing; as an objeft which
ought always to occupy a little remote
corner of his map of life; the ftudy of
which, though it is always to be poftponed,
is however not to be finally reje&ed;
which, though it cannot conveniently
come into his prefent fcheme of life, it is
intended fomehow or other to take up before death. This awful deception, this de-
fe& in the intelle&ual vifion, arifes, partly
from the bulk which the obje&s of time
and fenfe acquire in our eyes by their near-
nefs; while the invifible realities of eternity are but faintly difcerned by a feeble
faith,

faith, through a dim and diftant medium. It arifes alfo partly from a totally falfe idea of the nature of Chriftianity, from a fatal fancy that we can repent at any future period, and that as amendment is a thing which will always be in our own power, it will be time enough to think of reforming our life, when we fhould only think of clofing it.

But depend upon it, that a heart long hardened, I do not mean by grofs vices merely, but by a fondnefs for the world, by an habitual and exceffive indulgence in the pleafures of fenfe, will by no means be in a favourable ftate to admit the light of divine truth, or to receive the impreffions of divine grace. God indeed fometimes fhows us by an act of his fovereignty, that this wonderful change, the converfion of a finner's heart, may be produced without the intervention of human means, to fhow that the work is His. But as this is not the way in which the Almighty ufually deals with his creatures, it would be nearly

as prepofterous for men to act on this prefumption, and fin on in hopes of a mira-
culous converfion, as it would be to take
no means for the prefervation of our lives,
becaufe Jefus Chrift raifed Lazarus from
the dead.

CHAP. XI.

On the manner of inftructing young perfons in Religion.—General remarks on the genius of Chriftianity.

I WOULD now with great deference addrefs thofe refpectable characters who are really concerned about the beft interefts of their children; thofe to whom Chriftianity is indeed an important confideration, but whofe habits of life have hitherto hindered them from giving it its due degree in the fcale of education.

Begin then with confidering that religion is a part, and the moft prominent part, in your fyftem of inftruction. Do not communicate its principles in a random defultory way; nor fcantily ftint this bufinefs to only fuch fcraps and remnants

of

of time as may be cafually picked up from the gleanings of other acquirements. " Will you bring to God for a facrifice " that which cofts you nothing ?" Let the beft part of the day, which with moft people is the earlieft part, be fteadily and invariably dedicated to this work by your children, before they are tired with their other ftudies, while the intellect is clear, the fpirits light, and the attention unfatigued.

Confine not your inftructions to mere verbal rituals and dry fyftems ; but inftruct them in a way which fhall intereft their feelings ; by lively images, and by a warm practical application of what they read to their own hearts and circumftances. If you do not ftudy the great but too much flighted art of fixing, of commanding, of chaining the attention, you may throw away much time and labour, with little other effect than that of difgufting your pupil and wearying yourfelf. There feems to be no good reafon that while every
other

other thing is to be made amufing, religion
alone muft be dry and uninviting. Do not
fancy that a thing is good merely becaufe
it is dull. Why fhould not the moft entertaining powers of the human mind be
fupremely confecrated to that fubject which
is moft worthy of their full exercife? The
misfortune is, that religious learning is too
often rather confidered as an act of the
memory than of the heart and feelings; and that children are turned over to
the dry work of getting by rote as a tafk
that which they fhould get from example
and animated converfation, from lively
difcuffion, in which the pupil fhould learn
to bear a part. Teach them rather, as
their Bleffed Saviour taught, by interefting parables, which, while they corrected
the heart, left fome exercife for the ingenuity in the folution, and for the feelings
in their application. Teach, as HE taught,
by feizing on furrounding objects, paffing
events, local circumftances, peculiar cha-

6   racters,

racters, apt allufions, juft analogy, appropriate illuftration.   Call in all creation,
animate and inanimate, to your aid, and
accuftom your young audience to

Find tongues in trees, books in the running brooks,
Sermons in ftones, and good in every thing.

Even when the nature of your fubject
makes it neceffary for you to be more
plain and didactic, do not fail frequently to
enliven thefe lefs engaging parts of your
difcourfe with fome incidental imagery
which fhall captivate the fancy.   Relieve
what would otherwife be too dry and pre-
ceptive, with fome ftriking exemplification
in point, fome touching inftance to be imitated, fome awful warning to be avoided;
fomething which fhall illuftrate your inftruction, which fhall realize your pofition,
which fhall embody your idea, and give
fhape and form, colour and life, to your
precept.   Endeavour unremittingly to connect the reader with the fubject, by making
her feel that what you teach is neither an
abftract

abftract truth, nor a thing of mere general information, but that it is a bufinefs in which *fhe herfelf* is individually and immediately concerned; in which not only her eternal falvation but her *prefent* happinefs is involved. Do, according to your meafure of ability, what the Holy Spirit which indited the Scriptures has done, always take the fenfibility of the learner into your account of the faculties which are to be worked upon. " For the doc-" trines of the Bible," as the profound and enlightened Bacon obferves, " are not " propofed to us in a naked logical form, " but arrayed in the moft beautiful and " ftriking colours which creation affords." By thofe affecting illuftrations ufed by Him " who knew what was in man," and therefore beft knew how to addrefs him, it was, that the unlettered audiences of Chrift and his Apoftles were enabled both to comprehend and to relifh doctrines, which would not readily have made their way to their underftandings, had they not

firft

firft touched their hearts; and which
would have found accefs to neither the one
nor the other, had they been delivered in
dry fcholaftic difquifitions. Now thofe
audiences not being learned, may be fuppofed to have been nearly in the ftate of
children, as to their receptive faculties, and
to have required nearly the fame fort of inftruction; that is, they were more capable
of being affected with what was fimple,
and touching, and lively, than what was
elaborate, abftrufe, and unaffecting. Heaven and earth were made to furnifh their
contributions, when man was to be taught
that fcience which was to make him wife
unto falvation. If that be the pureft eloquence which moft perfuades, and which
comes home to the heart with the fulleft
evidence and the moft irrefiftible force,
then no eloquence is fo powerful as that of
Scripture: and an intelligent Chriftian
teacher will be admonifhed by the mode of
Scripture itfelf, how to communicate its
truths with life and fpirit; " while he is
                                    " mufing,

" mufing, the fire burns :" that fire which
will preferve him from an infipid and freez-
ing mode of inftruction. He will moreover, as was faid above, always carefully
keep up a quick fenfe of the perfonal intereft the pupil has in every religious inftruction which is impreffed upon him.
He will teach as Paul prayed, " with the
" fpirit, and with the underftanding alfo;"
and in imitating this great model, he will
neceffarily avoid the oppofite faults of two
different forts of inftructors ; for while
fome of our divines of the higher clafs
have been too apt to preach as if mankind
had only intellect, and the lower and more
popular fort as if they had only paffions,
do you borrow what is good from both,
and addrefs your pupils as beings compounded of both underftanding and affections *:

Fancy

---

* The zeal and diligence with which the Bifhop of
London's weekly lectures have been attended by perfons of all ranks and defcriptions, but more efpecially

Fancy not that the Bible is too difficult and intricate to be prefented in its own naked form, and that it puzzles and bewilders the youthful underftanding. In all needful and indifpenfable points of knowledge, the darknefs of Scripture, as a great Chriftian philofopher * has obferved, " is but a partial darknefs, like that of " Egypt, which benighted only the enemies " of God, while it left his children in clear " day." It is not pretended that the Bible will *find* in the reader clear views of God and of Chrift, of the foul and eternity, but that it will *give* them. And if it be really the appropriate character of Scrip-

---

by that clafs to whom this little work is addreffed, is a very promifing circumftance for the age. And while one confiders with pleafure the advantages peculiarly to be derived by the young from fo interefting and animated an expofition of the Gofpel, one is further led to rejoice at the countenance given by fuch high authority to the revival of that excellent, but too much neglected practice of lectures.

* Mr. Boyle.

ture,

ture, as it tells us itself that it is, " to en-
" lighten the eyes of the *blind*," and " to
" make wife the *simple*," then it is as well
calculated for the youthful and uninformed
as for any other clafs ; and as it was never
expected that the greater part of Chriftians
fhould be learned, fo is learning. though
of ineftimable value in a teacher of theo-
logy, no *effential* qualification for a common Chriftian: for which reafon Scripture
truths are expreffed with that clear and
fimple evidence adapted to the kind of
affent which they require ; an affent materially different from that fort of demon-
ftration which a mathematical theorem demands. He who could bring an unprejudiced heart and an unperverted will,
would bring to the Scriptures the beft
qualification for underftanding and receiv-
ing them. And though they contain
things which the pupil cannot comprehend,
(as what ancient poet, hiftorian, or orator
does not,) the teacher may addrefs to him
the words which Chrift addreffed to Peter,

s 2 " What

" What I do thou knoweſt not now, but
" thou ſhalt know hereafter."

Young people who have been taught re
ligion in a formal and ſuperficial way, who
have had all its drudgeries and none of its
pleaſures, will probably have acquired ſo
little reliſh for it, as to conſider the continued proſecution of their religious ſtudies
as a badge of their tutelage, as a mark
that they are ſtill under ſubjection ; and
will look forward with impatience to the
hour of their emancipation from the lectures on Chriſtianity, as the æra of their
promiſed liberty. They will long for the
period when its leſſons ſhall ceaſe to be delivered ; will conclude that, having once
attained ſuch an age, and arrived at the
required proficiency, the object will be
accompliſhed and the labour at an end.
But let not *your* children " ſo learn Chriſt."
Apprize them that no ſpecific day will ever
arrive on which they ſhall ſay, I *have* attained ; but inform them, that every acquiſition muſt be followed up ; knowledge
muſt

muſt be increaſed; prejudices ſubdued;
good habits rooted; evil ones eradicated;
diſpoſitions ſtrengthened; principles confirmed; till, going on from light to light,
and from ſtrength to ſtrength, they come
" to the meaſure of the ſtature of the ful-
" neſs of Chriſt."

But though ſerious inſtruction will not
only be unintereſting but irkſome if conveyed to youth in a cold didactic way, yet
if their affections are ſuitably engaged,
while their underſtandings are kept in exerciſe, their hearts, ſo far from neceſſarily
revolting, as ſome inſiſt, will often receive
the moſt ſolemn truths with alacrity. It is,
as we have repeated, the manner which revolts them, and not the thing.

As it is notorious that men of wit and
ſprightly fancy have been the moſt formidable enemies to Chriſtianity; while men, in
whom thoſe talents have been conſecrated
to God, have been ſome of her moſt uſeful
champions, take particular care to preſs
that ardent and ever-active power, the

s 3   *imagination*

imagination, into the fervice of religion;
this bright and bufy faculty will be leading its poffeffor into perpetual peril, and is
an enemy of peculiar potency till it come
to be employed in the caufe of God.   It
is a lion, which though worldly prudence
indeed may *chain* fo as to prevent outward
mifchief, yet the malignity remains within;
but when fanctified by Chriftianity, the
imagination is a lion *tamed;* you have all
the benefit of its ftrength and its activity,
divefted of its mifchief.   God never beftowed that noble but reftlefs faculty,
without intending it to be an inftrument of
his own glory; though it has been too
often fet up in rebellion againft him; becaufe, in its youthful ftirrings, while all alive
and full of action, it has not been feized
upon to fight for its rightful Sovereign,
but was early enlifted with little oppofition
under the banners of the world, the flefh,
and the devil.   Religion is the only fubject
in which, under the guidance of a fevere
and fober-minded prudence, this difcurfive
faculty

faculty can fafely ftretch its powers and expand its energies. But let it be remembered, that it muft be a found and genuine Chriftianity which can alone fo chaftife and regulate the imagination, as to reftrain it from thofe errors and exceffes into which a falfe, a miftaken, an irregular religion, has too often led its injudicious and ill-inftructed profeffor. Some of the moft fatal extremes into which a wild enthufiafm or a frightful fuperftition has plunged its unhappy votaries, have been owing to the want of a due direction, of a ftrict and holy caftigation of this ever-working faculty. To fecure imagination therefore on the fafe fide, and, if I may change the metaphor, to put it under the direction of its true pilot in the ftormy voyage of life, is like engaging thofe potent elements, the wind and tide, in your favour.

In your communications with young people, take care to convince them that as religion is not a bufinefs to be laid afide with the leffon, fo neither is it a fingle branch of duty; fome detached thing, which

like

like the acquisition of an art or a language, is to be practised separately, and to have its distinct periods and modes of operation. But let them understand, that common acts, by the spirit in which they are to be performed, are to be made acts of religion; that Christianity may be considered as having something of that influence over the conduct which external grace has over the manners; for as it is not the performance of some particular act which denominates any one to be graceful, grace being a spirit diffused through the whole system, which animates every sentiment, and informs every action; as she who has true personal grace has it uniformly, and is not sometimes awkward and sometimes elegant; does not sometimes lay it down and sometimes take it up; so religion is not an occasional act, but an indwelling principle, an inwrought habit, a pervading and informing spirit, from which indeed every act derives all its life. and energy, and beauty.

Give

Give them clear views of the broad
difcrimination between practical religion
and worldly morality; in fhort, between the
virtues of Chriftians and of Pagans. Show
them that no good qualities are genuine but
fuch as flow from the religion of Chrift.
Let them learn that the virtues which the
better fort of people, who yet are deftitute
of true Chriftianity, inculcate and practife,
refemble thofe virtues which have the love
of God for their motive, juft as counterfeit
coin refembles fterling gold ; they may
have, it is true, certain points of refemblance with the others ; they may be
bright and fhining ; they have perhaps
the image and the fuperfcription, but they
ever want the true diftinguifhing properties;
they want fterling value, purity, and weight.
They may indeed pafs current in the traffic
of this world, but when brought to the
touchftone, they will be found full of alloy ;
when weighed in the balance of the
fanctuary, " they will be found wanting ;"
they will not ftand that final trial which

is

is to feparate " the precious from the
" vile;" they will not abide the day
" of *his* coming who is like a refiner's
" fire."

One error into which even fome good
people are apt to fall, is that of endeavouring to deceive young minds by temporifing
expedients.   In order to allure them
to become religious, they exhibit falfe,
or faint, or inadequate views of Chriftianity; and while they reprefent it as
it really is, as a life of fuperior happinefs
and advantage, they conceal its difficulties,
and like the Jefuitical Chinefe miffionaries,
extenuate, or fink, or deny, fuch parts of
it as are leaft alluring to human pride.
In attempting to difguife its principle, they
deftroy its efficacy.   But befides that, the
project fails with them as it did with the
Jefuits; all fraud is bad in itfelf; and a
pious fraud is a contradiction in terms
which ought to be buried in the rubbifh of
papal defolation,

Inftead

Inftead of reprefenting to the young Chriftian, that it may be poffible by a prudent ingenuity at once to purfue, with equal ardour and fuccefs, worldly fame and eternal glory, would it not be more honeft to tell him fairly and unambiguoufly that there are two diftinct roads between which there is a broad boundary line? that there are two contending and irreconcileable interefts? that he muft forfake the one if he would cleave to the other? that there are two forts of characters at eternal variance? that he muft renounce the one if he is in earneft for the other? that nothing fhort of abfolute decifion can make a confirmed Chriftian? Point out the different forts of promifes annexed to thefe different forts of characters. Confefs in the language of Chrift how the man of the world often obtains (and it is the natural courfe of human things) the recompence he feduloufly feeks. " Verily " I fay unto you they have their reward."

Explain

Explain the beatitudes on the other hand,
and unfold what kind of fpecific reward is
there individually promifed to its concomitant virtue.   Show your pupil that to that
" poverty of fpirit" to which the kingdom
of heaven is promifed, it would be in-
confiftent to expect that the recompence
of human commendation fhould be alfo
attached ; that to that " purity of heart"
to which the beatific vifion is annexed, it
would be unreafonable to fuppofe you can
unite the praife of licentious wits, or the
admiration of a catch-club.   Thefe will be
beftowed on their appropriate and cor-
refponding merits.   Do not inlift them
under falfe colours ; difappointment will
produce defertion.   Different forts of
rewards are attached to different forts of
fervices ; and while you truly affert that
religious ways are " ways of pleafantnefs,
" and all her paths are peace," take care
that you do not lead them to depend too
exclufively   on   worldly   happinefs   and
earthly

earthly peace, for thefe make no part
of the covenant; they may be fuperadded,
but they were never ftipulated in the
contract.

But if, in order to attract the young to a
religious courfe, you difingenuoufly conceal its difficulties, while you are enlarging
upon its pleafures, you will tempt them to
diftruft the truth of Scripture itfelf. For
what will they think, not only of a few
detached texts, but of the general caft and
colour of the Gofpel when contrafted with
your reprefentation of it? What notion
will they conceive of " the ftrait gate"
and " narrow way?" of the amputation of
a " right hand?" of the excifion of a
" right eye?" of the other ftrong meta-
phors by which the Chriftian warfare
is fhadowed out? of " crucifying the
" flefh?" of " mortifying the old man?"
of " dying unto fin?" of " overcoming
" the world?" Do you not think their
meek and compaffionate Saviour who died
for your children loved them as well as
                                          you

you love them ?   And if this were his language, ought it not to be yours ?   It is the
language of true love ; of that love with
which a merciful God loved the world,
when he fpared not his own Son.   Do
not then try to conceal from them, that
the life of a Chriftian is neceffarily oppofite
to the life of the world; and do not feek,
by a vain attempt at accommodation,
to reconcile that difference which Chrift
himfelf has pronounced to be irreconcileable.

May it not be partly owing to the want
of a due introduction to the knowledge of
the real nature and fpirit of religion, that
fo many young Chriftians, who fet out in
a fair and flourifhing way, decline and
wither when they come to perceive the
requifitions of experimental Chriftianity ?
requifitions which they had not fufpected
of making any part of the plan ; and from
which, when they afterwards difcover them,
they fhrink back, as not prepared for the
unexpected conteft.

People

People are no more to be cheated into
religion than into learning. The fame
fpirit which influences your oath in a court
of juftice fhould influence your difcourfe in
that court of equity—your family. Your
children fhould be told the truth, the
whole truth, and nothing but the truth.
It is unneceffary to add, that it muft
be done gradually and difcreetly. We
know whofe example we have for poft-
poning that which the mind is not yet prepared to receive : " I have many things
" yet to fay to you, but ye cannot bear
" them *now*." Accuftom them to reafon
by analogy. Explain to them that great
worldly attainments are never made without great facrifices; that the merchant
cannot become rich without induftry; the
ftatefman eminent without labour; the
fcholar learned without ftudy; the hero
renowned without danger : would it not
then, on human principles, be unreafonable to think that the Chriftian alone
fhould obtain a triumph without a warfare?

the

the higheſt prize with the loweſt exertions?
an eternal crown without a preſent croſs?
and that heaven is the only reward which
the idle may reckon upon?   No: though
ſalvation " be the *gift* of God," yet it muſt
be " *worked out*."   Convince your young
friends, however, that in this caſe the difficulty of the battle bears no proportion to
the prize of the victory.   In one reſpect,
indeed, the point of reſemblance fails, and
that moſt advantageouſly for the Chriſtian ;
for while, even by the moſt probable
means, which are the union of talents with
diligence, no human proſperity can be in-
ſured to the worldly candidate ; while the
moſt ſuccefsful adventurer may fail by the
fault of another ; while the beſt concerted
project of the ſtateſman may be cruſhed ;
the braveſt hero loſe the battle ; the
brighteſt genius fail of getting bread ; and
while, moreover, the pleaſure ariſing even
from ſuccefs in theſe may be no ſooner
taſted than it is poiſoned by a more pro-
                                                   ſperous

fperous rival; the perfevering Chriftian is
fafe and certain of obtaining *his* object;
no misfortunes can defeat *his* hope; no
competition can endanger *his* fuccefs; for
though another gain, he will not lofe;
nay, the fuccefs of another, fo far from diminifhing his gain, is an addition to it; the
more he diffufes, the richer he grows; his
bleffings are enlarged by communication ;
and that mortal hour which cuts off for
ever the hopes of worldly men, crowns
and confummates his.

Beware at the fame time of fetting up
any act of felf-denial or mortification as
the *procuring* caufe of falvation. This
would be a prefumptuous project to *pur-
chafe* that eternal life which is declared to
be the " free *gift* of God." This would
be to fend your children, not to the Gofpel
to learn their Chriftianity, but to the
Monks and Afcetics of the middle ages ;
it would be fending them to Peter the
Hermit, and the holy fathers of the Defert,
and not to Peter the Apoftle and his

Divine

Divine Mafter. Mortification is not the
price; it is nothing more than the difcipline of a foul of which fin is the difeafe,
the diet prefcribed by the great phyfician.
Without this guard the young devout
Chriftian would be led to fancy that
abftinence, pilgrimage, and penance might
be adopted as the cheap fubftitute for the
fubdued defire, the refifted temptation,
the conquered corruption, and the obedient will; and would be almoft in as
much danger, on the one hand, of felf-
righteoufnefs arifing from aufterities and
mortification, as fhe would be, on the
other, from felf-gratification in the indulgences of the world. And while you
carefully imprefs on her the neceffity of
living a life of ftrict obedience if fhe would
pleafe God, do not neglect to remind her
alfo that a complete renunciation of her
own performances as a ground of merit,
purchafing the favour of God by their own
intrinfic worth, is included in that obedience.

It

It is of the laſt importance, in ſtamping on young minds a true impreſſion of the genius of Chriſtianity, to poſſeſs them with a conviction that it is the purity of the motive which not only gives worth and beauty, but which, in a Chriſtian ſenſe, gives life and ſoul to the beſt action: nay, that while a right intention will be acknowledged and accepted at the final judgment, even without the act, the act itſelf will be diſowned which wanted the baſis of a pure deſign. " Thou didſt " well that it was in thy *heart* to build " me a temple," ſaid the Almighty to that Monarch whom yet he permitted not to build it. How many ſplendid actions will be rejected in the great day of retribution, to which ſtatues and monuments have been raiſed on earth, while their almoſt deïfied authors ſhall be as much confounded at their own unexpected repro‐ bation, as at the divine acceptance of thoſe " whoſe life the world counted madneſs."

It

It is worthy of remark, that "Depart from
" me, I never knew you," is not the ma-
lediction denounced on the fceptic or the
fcoffer, but on the high profeffor, on the
unfruitful worker of " miracles," on the
unfanctified utterer of " prophecies;" for
even acts of piety wanting the purifying
principle, however they may dazzle men,
offend God.   Cain facrificed, Balaam pro-
phefied, Rouffeau wrote the moft fublime
panegyric on the *Son of Mary*, VOLTAIRE
BUILT A CHURCH! nay, fo fuperior was
his affectation of fanctity, that he often-
tatioufly declared, that while others were
raifing churches to *Saints*, there was one
man at leaft who would erect his church
to *God* * : that God whofe altars he was
overthrowing, whofe name he was vilify·
ing, whofe gofpel he was exterminating,
and the very name of whofe Son he had

---

* *Deo erexit Voltaire*, is the infcription affixed by
himfelf on his church at Ferney.

folemnly

folemnly pledged himfelf to blot from the face of the earth!

Though it be impoffible here to enumerate all thofe Chriftian virtues which fhould be impreffed in the progrefs of a Chriftian education, yet in this connection I cannot forbear mentioning one which more immediately grows out of the fubject; and to remark that the principle which fhould be the invariable concomitant of all inftruction, and efpecially of religious inftruction, is humility. As this temper is inculcated in every page of the Gofpel; as it is deducible from every precept and every action of Chrift; that is a fufficient intimation that it fhould be made to grow out of every ftudy, that it fhould be grafted on every acquifition. It is the turning point, the leading principle indicative of the very genius, of the very being of Chriftianity. This chaftifing quality fhould therefore be conftantly

made

made in education to operate as the only counteraction of that " knowledge which " puffeth up." Youth fhould be taught that as humility is the difcriminating characteriftic of our religion, therefore a proud Chriftian, a haughty difciple of a crucified Mafter, furnifhes perhaps a ftronger oppofition in terms than the whole compafs of language can exhibit. They fhould be taught that humility being the appropriate grace of Chriftianity, is precifely the thing which makes Chriftian and Pagan virtues *effentially* different. The virtues of the Romans, for inftance, were obvioufly founded in pride; as a proof of this, they had not even a word in their copious language to exprefs humility, but what was ufed in a bad fenfe, and conveyed the idea of meannefs or vilenefs, of bafenefs and fervility. Chriftianity fo ftands on its own fingle ground, is fo far from affimilating itfelf to the fpirit of other religions, that, unlike the Roman Emperor, who though

he

he would not become a Chriftian, yet or-
dered that the image of Chrift fhould be
fet up in the Pantheon with thofe of the
heathen gods, and be worfhipped in common with them; Chriftianity not only
rejeَcts all fuch partnerfhips with other religions, but it pulls down their images, de-
faces their temples, tramples on their ho-
nours, founds its own exiftence on the
ruins of fpurious religions and fpurious
virtues, and will be every thing when it
is admitted to be any thing.

Will it be going too much out of the
way to obferve, that Chriftian Britain
retaliates upon Pagan Rome? For if the
former ufed humility in a bad fenfe, has
not latter learnt to ufe pride in a good
one? May we without impertinence, venture to remark, that, in the deliberations
of as honourable and upright political af-
femblies as ever adorned, or, under Providence, upheld a country; in orations
which leave us nothing to envy in Attic or

T 4   Roman

Roman eloquence in their beſt days : it
were to be wiſhed that we did not borrow
from Rome an epithet which ſuited the
genius of her religion, as much as it
militates againſt that of ours ?   The pane-
gyriſt of the battle of Marathon, of Platea,
or of Zama, might with propriety ſpeak of
a " proud day," or a " proud event," or
a " proud ſucceſs."   But ſurely the
Chriſtian encomiaſts of the battle of the
Nile might, from their abundance, ſeleἀ an
epithet better appropriated to ſuch a
viἀory—a viἀory which, by preſerving
Europe, has perhaps preſerved that religion
which ſets its foot on the very neck of
pride, and in which the conqueror himſelf,
even in the firſt ardors of triumph, forgot
not to aſcribe the viἀory to ALMIGHTY
GOD.   Let us leave to the enemy both the
term and the thing; arrogant words being
the only weapons in which we muſt ever
vail to their decided ſuperiority.   As we
muſt deſpair of the viἀory, let us diſdain
the conteſt.

Above

Above all things then you fhould beware
that your pupils do not take up with
a vague, general, and undefined religion ;
but look to it that their Chriftianity be
really the religion of Chrift. Inftead of
flurring over the doctrines of the Crofs, as
difreputable appendages to our religion,
which are to be difguifed or got over as
well as we can, but which are never to be
dwelt upon, take care to make thefe your
grand fundamental articles. Do not di-
lute, or explain away thefe doctrines, and
by fome elegant periphrafis *hint* at a Saviour, inftead of making him the foundation ftone of your fyftem. Do not convey primary, and plain, and awful, and indifpenfable truths elliptically, I mean as
fomething that is to be underftood without
being expreffed ; nor ftudy fafhionable
circumlocutions to avoid names and things
on which our falvation hangs, in order to
prevent your difcourfe from being offenfive. Perfons who are thus inftructed
in religion with more good-breeding than
                                    ferioufnefs

ferioufnefs and fimplicity, imbibe a diftafte
for plain fcriptural language; and the
Scriptures themfelves are fo little in ufe
with a certain fafhionable clafs of readers,
that when the doctrines and language of
the Bible occafionally occur in other authors, or in converfation, they prefent a
fort of novelty and peculiarity which offend; and fuch readers as difufe the Bible
are apt, from a fuppofed delicacy of tafte,
to call that precife and puritanical which
is in fact found and fcriptural. Nay, it has
feveral times happened to the author to
hear perfons of fenfe and learning ridicule
infulated fentiments and expreffions that
have fallen in their way, which they would
have treated with decent refpect had they
known them to be, as they really were,
texts of Scripture. This obfervation is
hazarded with a view to enforce the importance of early communicating religious
knowledge, and of infufing an early tafte
for the venerable phrafeology of Scripture.

The

The perfons in queftion thus poffeffing a kind of Pagan Chriftianity; are apt to acquire a fort of Pagan expreffion alfo, which juft enables them to fpeak with complacency of the " Deity," of a " firft " caufe," and of " confcience." Nay, fome may even go fo far as to talk of " the Founder of our religion," of the " Author of Chriftianity," in the fame general terms, as they would talk of the prophet of Arabia, or the lawgiver of China, of Athens, or of the Jews. But their refined ears revolt not a little at the unadorned name of Chrift ; and even the naked and unqualified term of our Saviour, or Redeemer, carries with it a queerifh, inelegant, not to fay a fufpicious found. They will exprefs a ferious difapprobation of what is wrong, under the moral term of *vice*, or the forenfic term of *crime;* but they are apt to think that the Scripture term of *fin* has fomething fanatical in it ; and, while they
discover

difcover a great refpeᴄt for morality, they
do not much relifh holinefs, which is indeed the fpecific and only morality of a
Chriftian. They will fpeak readily of a
man's reforming, or leaving off a vicious
habit, or growing more correᴄt in fome
individual praᴄtice; but the idea conveyed
under any of the Scripture phrafes figni-
fying a total change of heart, they would
ftigmatize as the very fhibboleth of a feᴄt,
though it is the language of a Liturgy they
affeᴄt to admire, and of a Gofpel which
they profefs to receive.

CHAP. XII.

*Hints suggested for furnishing young persons
with a scheme of prayer.*

THOSE who are aware of the ineftimable
value of prayer themfelves, will naturally
be anxious not only that this duty fhould
be earneftly inculcated on their children,
but that they fhould be taught it in
the beft manner; and *fuch* parents need
little perfuafion or counfel on the fubject.
Yet children of decent and orderly (I will
not fay of ftrictly religious) families are
often fo fuperficially inftructed in this
important bufinefs, that it is not unufual,
when they are afked what prayers they
ufe, to anfwer, " the Lord's Prayer and
" the *Creed*." And even fome who are
better taught, are not always made to
underftand with fufficient clearnefs the

fpecific

fpecific diftinction between the two; that
the one is the confeffion of their *faith*,
and the other the model for their *fup-
plications*. By this confufed and indiftinct
beginning, they fet out with a perplexity
in their ideas, which is not always
completely difentangled in more advanced
life.

An intelligent mother will feize the firft
occafion which the child's opening underftanding fhall allow, for making a little
courfe of lectures on the Lord's Prayer,
taking every divifion or fhort fentence
feparately; for each furnifhes valuable materials for a diftinct lecture. The child
fhould be led gradually through every part
of this divine compofition; fhe fhould
be taught to break it into all the regular
divifions, into which indeed it fo naturally
refolves itfelf. She fhould be made to
comprehend one by one each of its fhort
but weighty fentences; to amplify and
fpread them out for the purpofe of better
underftanding them, not in their moft
extenfive

extensive and critical sense, but in their most simple and obvious meaning.   For in those condensed and substantial expressions, every word is an ingot, and will bear beating out; so that the teacher's difficulty will not so much be what she shall say as what she shall suppress; so abundant· is the expository matter which this succinct pattern suggests.

When the child has a pretty good conception of the meaning of each division, she should then be made to observe the connection, relation, and dependance of the several parts of this prayer one upon another; for there is great method and connection in it.   We pray that the "kingdom of God may come," as the best means to "hallow his name;" and that by us, the obedient subjects of his kingdom, "his will may be done."   A judicious interpreter will observe how logically and consequently one clause grows out of another, though she will use neither the word logical nor consequence; for all explana-

4   tions

tions fhould be made in the moft plain and
familiar terms, it being words, and not
things, which commonly perplex children,
if, as it fometimes happens, the teacher,
though not wanting fenfe, want perfpicuity
and fimplicity.

The young perfon, from being made
a complete miftrefs of this fhort compofition, (which as it is to be her guide and
model through life, too much pains cannot
be beftowed on it,) will have a clearer
conception, not only of its individual contents, but of prayer in general, than many
ever attain, though their memory has been
perhaps loaded with long and unexplained
forms, which they have been accuftomed to
fwallow in the lump without fcrutiny, and
without difcrimination. Prayer fhould not
be fo fwallowed. It is a regular prefcription, which fhould ftand analyfis and exa-
mination : it is not a charm, the fuccefsful
operation of which depends on your blindly
taking it, without knowing what is in it,
and in which the good you receive is promoted by your ignorance of its contents.

I would

I would have it underſtood that by theſe little comments, I do not mean that the child ſhould be put to learn dry, and to her unintelligible expoſitions; but that the expoſition is to be colloquial. And here I muſt remark in general, that the teacher is ſometimes unreaſonably apt to relieve herſelf at the child's expence, by loading the *memory* of a little creature on occaſions in which far other faculties ſhould be put in exerciſe. The child herſelf ſhould be made to furniſh a good part of this extemporaneous commentary by her anſwers; in which anſwers ſhe will be much aſſiſted by the judgment the teacher uſes in her manner of queſtioning. And the youthful underſtanding, when its powers are properly ſet at work, will ſoon ſtrengthen by exerciſe, ſo as to furniſh reaſonable if not very correct anſwers.

Written forms of prayer are not only uſeful and proper, but indiſpenſably neceſſary to begin with. But I will hazard the remark, that if children are thrown *excluſively* on the beſt forms, if they are made to commit them to memory like a copy of verfes, and to repeat them in a dry, cuftomary way, they will produce little effect on their minds. They will not underftand what they repeat, if we do not early open to them the important *fcheme* of prayer. Without fuch an elementary introduction to this duty, they will afterwards be either ignorant or enthufiafts, or both. We fhould give them *knowledge* before we can expect them to make much progrefs in *piety*, and as a due preparative to. it: Chriftian inftruction in this refembling the fun, who, in the courfe of his communications, gives light before he gives heat. And to labour to excite a fpirit of devotion without firft infufing that knowledge out of which it is to grow, is practically reviving the popifh maxim, that Ignorance is the mother of Devotion, and virtually adopting the popifh rule, of praying in an unknown tongue.

Children, let me again obferve, will not attend to their prayers if they do not underftand them ; and they will not underftand them, if they are not taught to

analyfe.

analyfe, to diffect them, to know their
component parts, and to methodife them.

It is not enough to teach them to confider prayer under the general idea that it
is an application to God for what they
want, and an acknowledgment to Him for
what they have.   This, though true in the
grofs, is not fufficiently precife and correct.
They fhould learn to define and to arrange
all the different parts of prayer.   And as
a preparative to prayer itfelf, they fhould
be impreffed with as clear an idea as their
capacity and the nature of the fubject admit, of " HIM with whom they have to
" do."   His omniprefence is perhaps, of
all his attributes, that of which we may
make the firft practical ufe.   Every head
of prayer is founded on fome great fcriptural truths, which truths the little analyfis
here fuggefted will materially affift to fix in
their minds.

On the knowledge that " God is,"
that he is an infinitely holy Being, and
that " he is the rewarder of all them that
" diligently feek him," will be grounded

the

the firſt part of prayer, which is *adoration.* The creature devoting itſelf to the Creator, or *ſelf-dedication,* next preſents itſelf.   And if they are firſt taught that important truth, that as needy creatures they want help; which may be done by ſome eaſy analogy, they will eaſily be led to underſtand how naturally *petition* forms a moſt conſiderable branch of prayer : and divine grace being among the things for which they are to petition, this naturally ſuggeſts to the mind the doctrine of the influences of the Holy Spirit.   And when to this is added the conviction, which will be readily worked into an ingenuous mind, that as offending creatures they want pardon, the neceſſity of *confeſſion* will eaſily be made intelligible to them.   But they ſhould be brought to underſtand that it muſt not be ſuch a general and vague confeſſion as awakens no ſenſe of perſonal humiliation, as excites no recollection of their own more peculiar and individual faults.   But it muſt be a confeſſion founded on ſelf-knowledge, which is itſelf to ariſe out of the practice of ſelf-examination : for want of this ſort

9   of

of difcriminating habit, a well-meaning but ill-inftructed girl may catch herfelf confefling the fins of fome other perfon, and omitting thofe which are more efpecially her own. On the gladnefs of heart natural to youth, it will be lefs difficult to imprefs the delightful duty of *thankf-giving*, which forms fo confiderable a branch of prayer. In this they fhould be habituated to recapitulate not only their general, but to enumerate their peculiar, daily, and incidental mercies, in the fame fpecific manner as they fhould have been taught to detail their *wants* in the petitionary, and their *faults* in the confeffional part. The fame warmth of feeling which will more readily difpofe them to exprefs their gratitude to God in thankfgiving, will alfo lead them more gladly to exprefs their love to their parents and friends, by adopting another indifpenfable, and to an affectionate heart, pleafing part of prayer, which is *interceffion*.

When they have been made, by a plain and perfpicuous mode of inftruction, fully

to underſtand the different nature of all
theſe; and when they clearly comprehend
that *adoration, ſelf-dedication, confeſſion,
petition, thankſgiving,* and *interceſſion,* are
diſtinct heads, which muſt not be involved
in each other, you may exemplify the rules
by pointing out to them theſe ſucceſſive
branches in any well written form.   And
they will eaſily diſcern, that aſcription of
glory to that God to whom we owe ſo
much, and on whom we ſo entirely depend, is the concluſion into which a
Chriſtian's prayer will naturally reſolve itſelf.   It is hardly needful to remind the
teacher that our truly Scriptural Liturgy
invariably furniſhes the example of preſent-
ing *every* requeſt in the name of the great
Mediator.   In the Liturgy too they will
meet with the beſt exemplifications of
prayers, exhibiting ſeparate ſpecimens of
each of the diſtinct heads we have been
ſuggeſting.

But in order that the minds of young
perſons may, without labour or difficulty,

be

be gradually brought into fuch a ftate of preparation as to be benefited by fuch a little courfe of lectures as we have recommended; they fhould, from the time when they were firft able to read, have been employing themfelves at their leifure hours, in laying in a ftore of provifion for their prefent demands. And here the memory may be employed to good purpofe ; for being the firft faculty which is ripened, and which is indeed perfected when the others are only beginning to unfold themfelves, this is an intimation of Providence that it fhould be the firft feized on for the beft ufes. It fhould therefore be devoted to lay in a ftock of the more eafy and devotional parts of Scripture. The Pfalms alone are an inexhauftible ftore-houfe of rich materials *.

Children

* This will be fo far from fpoiling the cheer-fulnefs, or impeding the pleafures of childhood, that the author knows a little girl who, before fhe was feven years old, had learnt the whole Pfalter through a fecond time; and that without any

dimi-

Children whofe minds have been early
well furnifhed from thefe, will be competent at nine or ten years old to produce
from them, and to felect with no con-
temptible judgment fuitable examples of
all the parts of prayer ; and will be able
to extract and appropriate texts under each
refpective head, fo as to exhibit, without
help, complete fpecimens of every part
of prayer.   By confining them entirely to
the fenfe, and nearly to the words of
Scripture, they will be preferved from
enthufiafm, from irregularity, and conceit.
By being obliged continually to apply for
themfelves, they will get a habit in all
their difficulties of " fearching the Scrip-
" tures," which may be ufeful to them on
future and more trying occafions.   But I
would at firft *confine* them to the Bible ;
for were they allowed with equal freedom

---

diminution of uncommon gaiety of fpirits, or any
interference with the elegant acquirements fuited to
her ftation.

to

to ranfack other books with a view to get helps to embellifh their little com-pofitions, or rather compilations, they might be tempted to pafs off for their own what they pick up from others, which might tend at once to make them both vain and deceitful. This is a temptation to which they are too much laid open when they get extravagantly commended for any pilfered paffage with which they decorate their little themes and letters. But in the prefent inftance there is no danger of any fimilar deception, for there is fuch a facred fignature ftamped on every Scripture phrafe, that the owner's name can never be defaced or torn off from the goods, either by fraud or violence.

It would be well, if in thofe Pfalms which chidren were firft directed to get by heart, an eye were had to this their future application; and that they were employed, but without any intimation of your fubfequent defign, in learning fuch as may be beft turned to this account.

In

In the hundred and thirty-ninth, the firſt great truth to be imprinted on the young heart, the divine omnipreſence, as was before obſerved, is unfolded with ſuch a mixture of majeſtic grandeur, and ſuch an intereſting variety of intimate and local circumſtances, as is likely to ſeize on the quick and lively feelings of youth. The awful idea that that Being whom ſhe is taught to reverence, is not only *in general* " acquainted with all her ways," but that " he is about her path, and about " her bed," beſtows ſuch a ſenſe of real and preſent exiſtence on *him* of whom ſhe is apt to conceive as having his diſtant habitation only in Heaven, as will greatly help her to realize the ſenſe of his actual preſence.

The hundred and third Pſalm will open to the mind rich and abundant ſources of expreſſion for gratitude and thankſgiving, and it includes ſpiritual as well as temporal favours. It illuſtrates the compaſſionate

mercies

mercies of God by familiar and domeſtic images, of ſuch peculiar tenderneſs and exquiſite endearment, as are calculated to ſtrike upon every chord of filial fondneſs in the heart of an affectionate child. The fifty-firſt ſupplies an infinite variety of matter in whatever relates to confeſſion of ſin, or to ſupplication for the aids of the Spirit. The twenty-third abounds with captivating expreſſions of the protecting goodneſs and tender love of their heavenly Father, conveyed by paſtoral imagery of uncommon beauty and ſweetneſs: in ſhort, the greater part of theſe charming compoſitions overflows with materials for every head of prayer.

The child who, while ſhe was engaged in learning theſe Scriptures, was not aware that there was any ſpecific object in view, or any farther end to be anſwered by it, will afterwards feel an unexpected pleaſure ariſing from the application of her petty labours, when ſhe is called to draw out from her little treaſury of knowledge the

ſtores

ftores fhe has been infenfibly collecling;
and will be pleafed to find that without
any frefh applicaticn to ftudy, for fhe is
now obliged to exercife a higher faculty
than memory, fhe has lying ready in her
mind the materials with which fhe is at
length called upon to work. Her judgment muft be fet about feleching one
or two, or more texts which fhall contain the fubftance of every fpecific head
of prayer before noticed; and it will
be a farther exercife to her underftanding to concatenate the detached parts
into one regular whole, occafionally varying the arrangement as fhe likes; that
is, changing the order, fometimes beginning with invocation, fometimes with confeffion; fometimes dwelling longer on
one part, fometimes on another. As the
hardfhips of a religious Sunday are often
fo pathetically pleaded, as making one
of the heavy burdens of religion; and
as the friends of religion are fo often
called

called upon to mitigate its intolerable ri-
gours, might not fuch an exercife as has
been here fuggefted help, by varying its
occupations, to lighten its load ?

The habits of the pupil being thus
early formed, her memory, attention and
intellect being bent in a right direction,
and the exercife invariably maintained,
may one not reafonably hope that her
affections alfo, through divine grace, may
become interefted in the work, till fhe
will be enabled " to pray with the fpirit
" and with the underftanding alfo ?"
She will now be qualified to ufe a well-
compofed form with ferioufnefs and advantage ; for fhe will now ufe it not
mechanically, but rationally. That which
before appeared to her a mere mafs of
good words, will now appear a fignificant
compofition, exhibiting variety, and regu-
larity, and beauty ; and while fhe will
have the farther advantage of being enabled by her improved judgment to diftin-
guifh

guifh and felect for her own purpofe fuch prayers as are more judicious and more fcriptural, it will alfo habituate her to look for plan, and defign, and lucid order, in other works.

END OF THE FIRST VOLUME.

Lightning Source UK Ltd.
Milton Keynes UK
02 March 2011

168547UK00001B/46/P